The Family of Andrew Berry Anderson

By

Brian Keith Anderson

Addressing Any and All Hesitations

Andrew Berry

By

Brian Keith Anderson

"For Janice and Emil"

"Let love and faithfulness never leave you;
bind them around your neck,
write them on the tablet of your heart

"Then you will win favor and a good name
in the sight of God and man

— Proverbs 3:3–4

Your life together was a living testimony of this truth.

DEDICATION

"This volume is lovingly dedicated to **Janice Waleck.**"

She was the voice at the other end of Yahoo Chat, searching for Andrew Berry—before either of sus knew we were cousins. She walked cemeteries in Cowan and Winchester, chasing whispers and stone etchings. When she met me, Beth Anderson, and Saundra Anderson, we realized: we were kin through Peter Anderson Sr.

Together, we hunted lineage like treasure. We mapped it, lived it, traveled it. We shared files, built trees, hosted reunions, and made memories that stitched our branches together. Janice helped clean up the roots—and Emil, her devoted husband, rode up into the mountains until the day he did not return, he loved to ride a mountain bike on trails in Mountains. She followed a year later.

I tried to call. I searched. The obituaries found me first. And still, they are with me—

guiding every page I write. Janice and Emil: family by blood and by heart. Their names are a

blessing to me.

Copyright © 2025 Brian Keith Anderson

All rights reserved. No part of this book may be reproduced or transmitted in any form or by any means, electronic or mechanical, including photocopying, recording, or by any information storage and retrieval system, without the prior written permission of the publisher, except as permitted by law.

AI Disclosure: This work was written and created by the author. AI tools were used only for grammar, formatting, and organizational assistance. No AI was used to generate original text, images, or illustrations.

ISBN 979-8-9996886-1-3

First Edition – 2025

Printed in the United States of America by IngramSpark

Table of Contents

Chapter One 6

Chapter One (continued) 6

Chapter Two 6

Chapter Three 6

Chapter Four 6

Chapter Five 6

Chapter Six 6

Chapter Eight 7

Chapter Nine 7

Chapter One (continued) 25

Chapter Two 26

Chapter Three 28

Chapter Four 29

Chapter Five 30

Chapter Six 31

Chapter Seven 32

Chapter Eight 34

Chapter Nine 34

Chapter Ten 36

Chapter Eight, ... 75

Chapter Five, ... 75

Chapter Four, ... 75

Chapter Nine, ... 75

Chapter One, ... 75

Chapter Seven, ... 75

Chapter Ten, ... 76

Chapter Two, ... 76

Chapter Three, ... 76

Preface

This book began not as a task, but as a calling.

What started with scattered names and faded photographs soon became a sacred mission—a revival of memory, a reckoning with history, and a celebration of those who came before. Guided by conversations with Janice, Saundra, Beth, and my cousins in Texas, the search for identity grew roots deep into Appalachian soil and stretched through census pages, grave markers, and family lore.

Each document, each story uncovered, whispered the truth: our ancestors were more than entries in a ledger; they were dreamers, farmers, ministers, mothers, soldiers, and seekers. They built homes where there was none, sowed wheat, corn in faith, and bore the burdens of war and wilderness.

This volume is a tribute to them. With gratitude and reverence, I invite you to walk beside me through their lives and see reflections of your own.

The Family of Andrew Berry Anderson

Origins & Family Ties

He worked on the land and raised a family through decades of change.

This manuscript traces the descendants of Andrew Berry Anderson (1822–1899), born in Cowan, Franklin County, Tennessee, and laid to rest in Tekoa, Whitman County, Washington. He was one of many children of Peter Anderson Sr. (1765–1824) and Sinai Cynthia Roberts (1781–1874), whose legacy touched Tennessee, Georgia, Arkansas, Missouri, and Washington.

James Henry Anderson (1866–1957) ...and several others whose brief lives and early losses shaped the emotional terrain of this family's story.

It is through the grace of shared memory, prayerful research, and the work of cousins known and newly found that this lineage has been uncovered, refined, and preserved. The chapters to follow explore this family's journey with reverence and poetic care—honoring the names etched in stone and the voices that still echo in our lives.

Peter Anderson Sr. entered the world amid colonial uncertainty in New Sweden, Delaware—a place marked by deep Scandinavian roots. Baptized in Wilmington in 1766, his early life unfolded in proximity to rivers, trade routes, and tides of migration. Following family paths and opportunity, he eventually settled in Franklin County, Tennessee, where he would plant enduring roots.

Family & Legacy

Andrew Berry Anderson (1822–1899)

Peter's life became a landmark in and of itself—his burial in Cowan although unknown, is a testament to permanence, faith, and family.

Early Life & Family

Marriages & Family

Peter Jr.'s timeline is led by perseverance amid shifting family structures. His marital transitions and geographic mobility reflect both frontier uncertainty and resilience. The repetition of family names like "Elmore" and "Cordelia" hint at spiritual or ancestral tributes.

Peter Jr.'s name recurs through multiple counties and branches—a quiet patriarch whose descendants ripple into Coffee, McMinn, Montgomery, and beyond.

Descendants of Edward & Nancy

His sons William and George also perished in October 1862, marking this month as one of profound loss for the family.

This brutal act, cloaked as justice, claimed not only Edward but two of his sons, tearing through the Anderson family line with stunning force.

Origins & Family Ties

The fifth son of Peter Sr. and Sinai, William, was born in the shadow of the Cumberland foothills, amid the rhythm of a frontier life steeped in family and faith. His siblings stretched across Tennessee and beyond, each a thread in the expanding Anderson legacy.

His death in Bridgeport, Wise County is recorded among one of the darkest weeks for the Anderson family, and for justice denied.

The year 1862 brought heartbreak. Cornelious lost Edward Frost Anderson and William C. Anderson—two brothers swept up in the tragedy of the Great Hanging in Texas. Their deaths reverberated through family memory, and Cornelious's name stands beside theirs now in solemn kinship.

Cornelious's closing chapter unfolded in Bath County, Kentucky, far from the Cowan soil of his youth, yet still tethered to the Anderson story. His descendants lived on through farming, preaching, and quiet devotion—echoes of his steady spirit.

Born in Franklin County, Tennessee in 1819, this daughter of Peter Sr. and Sinai Cynthia Roberts entered the world between Mae (1814) and Andrew Berry (1822). Though her name is not preserved in surviving records, her birth situates her as the eighth child in a family shaped by faith, endurance, and sorrow.

Andrew Berry Anderson (9 April 1822 – 30 August 1899) Born in Cowan, Tennessee • Laid to rest in Tekoa, Washington

His descendants lived through war, westward expansion, and agricultural upheaval—each carrying names that paid homage to heritage: Columbus, Jackson, Washington, Frost.

Still, Andrew pressed forward, eventually settling in Tekoa, Washington, where he would end his days surrounded by family.

Andrew Berry Anderson may have wandered farther than any Anderson before him, but never aimlessly. His legacy is one of endurance, remembrance, and grace across geography.

Catherine was born in Cowan, Franklin County, Tennessee, the twelfth and final child of Peter Anderson Sr. and Sinai Cynthia Roberts. In 1843, she married Rev. Samuel Milton Tate (1820–1914), planting the roots of a family line that would come to define Tate Cove and the surrounding lands of Marion County.

She spent her life in Tennessee, raising children, enduring immense loss, and remaining a quiet pillar of faith and resilience through seven decades of family history.

Her children's names often echoed ancestral honor: Sinai Americus for her mother, Virginia and Tennessee for home soil, Knox, and McNalley for regional ties. The Tate family became woven into Marion County's spiritual, agricultural, and civic fabric.

They rolled again—not with creaking axles or dust-choked hooves, but with descendants in pickup trucks and sedans, tracing the century-old footsteps of their kin. The Anderson family reunion that summer marked 100 years since the original migration from Carthage, Missouri, to Latah County, Washington. It was a solemn caravan of remembrance, honoring the journey that Andrew Berry Anderson and Adeline Elizabeth undertook with grit, gospel hymns, and hand-sewn quilts folded beneath the stars.

The Chronicle captured the moment with ink and reverence: "Nearly a hundred descendants gathered today to commemorate the great Anderson trek—a testament to perseverance and pioneer spirit."

By sundown, they had shared stew, pie, and stories so vivid they stirred the dust. The article now clipped and yellowing, tucked in a family Bible, bore witness to the living roots still winding through eastern Washington soil.

Three years earlier, Andrew had been a farmer in Franklin, Tennessee, sowing crops, and dreams. Now he stood as a soldier returned, no longer cradling a plow but the silent testimony of battles survived. His service record, signed by Captain E. Isaac Rolfe, marked not just an end, but a beginning—the path back to soil, family, and peace.

The Anderson homestead saw no cannon fire, yet it bore the deepest wounds—three sons at war, but on opposing sides. Andrew Berry Anderson, the youngest of the trio, pledged himself to the Union cavalry. His two elder brothers joined the Confederacy, carrying Tennessee's cause with them into battlefields scarred by conviction and consequence.

"I remember the day they came," she said. "Yankee soldiers gave us fifteen minutes to gather what we could. My mother cried over the family clock, packed with jewelry and money. We tried to save it, but it burned with the house."

At forty-one, Andrew Berry Anderson was no fresh-faced recruit. Born in Franklin County, Tennessee, in 1822, he had already weathered the loss of two sons and two brothers to the war's toll. Yet on that summer day in Springfield, Missouri, he stepped forward and enlisted as a private in Company F of the 2nd Arkansas Union Cavalry—a regiment formed in defiance of secession, drawn from pockets of loyalty scattered across the Ozarks.

Adeline Elizabeth Dickens married Andrew Berry Anderson in Franklin County, Tennessee, in the spring of 1841. She was just sixteen, with dark eyes and a steady heart. Together, they would raise thirteen children—some born in Georgia, others in Arkansas, and still more in Missouri—each arrival marking another chapter in their westward migration.

Born in the mountain town of Blairsville, Georgia, Mary Ann Sina Anderson was the eldest daughter of Andrew Berry Anderson and Adeline Elizabeth Dickens. Her childhood was steeped in frontier rhythms—quilts stitched by candlelight, hymns sung in pinewood churches, and the slow westward pull of family migration.

She witnessed the Civil War as a young girl, losing three brothers—Cornelius, Andrew Jackson, and a second Cornelius—before their twelfth birthday. Her father fought for the Union, her uncles for the Confederacy. Through it all, Mary Ann remained a quiet anchor, helping her mother tend to the younger children and carry the family's faith forward.

In 1867, she married Thomas Jefferson Wimpy in Benton County, Arkansas. Together they raised a large family, with children born in Georgia, Arkansas, and Washington—each birth marking another step in the Anderson migration. By 1880, she had settled in Spangle, Washington, and later in Nez Perce County, Idaho, where she lived out her final decades.

Named for the explorer who crossed oceans, Christopher Columbus Anderson crossed a continent. Born in the Appalachian foothills of Union County, Georgia, he was the second child of Andrew Berry and Adeline Anderson. His early years were shaped by the rhythms of frontier life—plowing fields, tending livestock, and watching his family grow as they migrated westward.

By the 1860s, Christopher had witnessed as his sister the death of Cornelius and Andrew Jackson—during the Civil War years. He saw his father fight for the Union, while uncles stood with the Confederacy. Christopher himself would marry Salina C. Asbell in Missouri in 1866, and together they raised a large family across Missouri and Washington.

His life was one of quiet endurance—marked not by fame, but by family, labor, and legacy. And in this manuscript, I, Brian, he becomes more than a name. He becomes a bridge between generations.

Born in the shadow of the Civil War, Sarah J. Anderson was one of the earliest children of Andrew Berry and Adeline Elizabeth Anderson. Her birth in Arkansas marked the family's westward shift from Georgia, and her life would mirror the migration that defined the Anderson legacy.

She married George F. Huffman in Nez Perce County, Idaho, in 1880, and together they raised a family that would settle deep roots in the Pacific Northwest. Sarah lived through the deaths of her parents, her siblings, and the transformation of Tekoa from a frontier town to a settled community. She outlived all her siblings—including Mary Ann Sina, Christopher

Columbus, and George Washington Anderson—and bore witness to the passing of three Cornelius's brothers and Andrew Jackson, all lost young.

Sarah's final years were spent in Tekoa, where she died at the age of 105. Her burial in Goldenrod Cemetery placed her beside the very soil that her family helped pioneer. Her long life was marked not by headlines, but by endurance, grace, and the quiet rhythm of family.

Cornelius was the third child of Andrew Berry and Adeline Elizabeth Anderson, born in the red clay hills of Union County, Georgia. His early years were spent among the rhythms of a growing family—siblings arriving in quick succession, the household migrating westward through Arkansas and Missouri, chasing farmland and hope.

Though he never reached adulthood, Cornelius's name lives on in family memory. His parents would name another son Cornelius in 1852, only to lose him as well in 1864. These twin losses—two sons bearing the same name—speak to both grief and remembrance, a mother's longing, and a father's sorrow.

In your manuscript, Brian, Cornelius becomes more than a footnote. He becomes a symbol of the cost of war, the fragility of frontier life, and the enduring love of a family that carried his name westward.

John Morton Anderson was the sixth child of Andrew Berry and Adeline Elizabeth Anderson, born in the Appalachian foothills of Union County, Georgia. His early years were shaped by migration and mourning—three younger brothers lost during the Civil War, a father who fought for the Union, and a mother who held the family together through sorrow and soil.

He worked on the land, raised his family, and lived to see the deaths of all his siblings. His final years were spent in quiet reflection, surrounded by the legacy he helped build. On

Christmas Day, 1940, at the age of 91, John passed away in Rosalia. He was buried in the IOOF Evergreen Cemetery, close to the soil his family had tilled for generations.

Edward Frost Anderson was the fifth child of Andrew Berry and Adeline Elizabeth Dickens Anderson, born into a family already shaped by migration and mourning. His early years unfolded in Georgia and Arkansas, where he witnessed the loss of three younger brothers—Cornelius (twice) and Andrew Jackson—during the Civil War years. His father fought for the Union, his uncles for the Confederacy, and Edward grew up in the shadow of both conviction and consequence.

In 1871, Edward married Emma Elizabeth Bozarth in Benton County, Arkansas. Together they had several children before Emma's death in 1887. Two years later, Edward married Keturah Hannah Belle Masterson in Lewiston, Idaho, and their union produced a large family—fourteen children in total, born across Arkansas, Washington, and Idaho.

Born into the growing family of Andrew Berry and Adeline Elizabeth Dickens Anderson, Andrew Jackson was the sixth child and part of a generation shaped by frontier hardship and Civil War unrest. His birth in Arkansas marked a westward shift for the Andersons, who had left Georgia behind in search of new beginnings.

Though his life was short, Andrew's presence was felt among his siblings—Sarah Elizabeth, George Washington, Nancy Jane, and William Dawson—each of whom would live long lives and carry forward the family name. His death in 1863, at just ten years old, came during a time of national upheaval, and though the cause is unknown, the loss was surely felt deeply by his parents and siblings.

Andrew's memory lives quietly in the family tree, a reminder of the fragility of childhood in a turbulent era. His name, shared with a famous general and president, suggests the hopes his parents may have held for him—a life of strength, leadership, and legacy.

He worked on the land and raised a family through decades of change—from horse-drawn wagons to automobiles

The youngest son of Andrew Berry and Adeline Elizabeth Dickens Anderson, James Henry was born in Springfield, Missouri, as the family continued its westward journey. By age three, he was living in Benton County, Arkansas, and by his teens, he had settled in Spangle, Washington—part of the Anderson migration to the Inland Northwest.

In 1891, she married James Henry Anderson in Spokane, Washington. Together they raised a large family across Washington, Idaho, and Canada. Her children included:

Ernest was the firstborn of a large and scattered family, arriving in Tekoa just as the A Grace, Blanch, Hazel, Jessie, Geneva, and the twins Netta and Robby—as well as the quiet grief of lost infants: Lula B., Leila B., and unnamed brothers and sisters.

She migrated with the family to Saskatchewan and British Columbia, settling in Abbotsford where she lived out her final years

Blanch was born into a growing family, nestled between Grace and Hazel, and surrounded by both joy and sorrow. Her early years in Washington were marked by the births and losses of siblings—Lula B., Leila B., and an unnamed infant son—all of whom passed in infancy. She grew up alongside Hazel, Jessie, Geneva, and the twins Netta and Robby, forming a sisterhood that would stretch across borders.

Migration with the family to Saskatchewan, by the 1910s

Blanche's story is one of gentle continuity—no known children, but a life lived in the rhythm of family migrations and prairie seasons. Her name appears in family records as a steady presence, and her burial in Saskatoon places her among the northern Anderson branches.

Lula B. was born into the Anderson family during their years in Washington, nestled between Blanch and Hazel in birth order. Her arrival marked the eighth child of James and Narcissa, and her presence—though fleeting—was part of the rhythm of a family constantly on the move.

Her death in Revelstoke at just under two years old came during the family's northward migration, enroute to Saskatchewan. The cause is unknown, but the timing suggests hardship amid travel, illness, or the strain of frontier life.

Though Lula B. left no descendants, her name remains stitched into the Anderson quilt— an echo of innocence and loss. Her memory is honored alongside siblings who lived long lives and those, like Leila and the unnamed infants, whose stories were brief but sacred.

Migration with the family from Washington to Saskatchewan and eventually British Columbia

She was one of four infants lost to James and Narcissa—alongside Lula B., an unnamed son, and an unnamed daughter. These little lights, though fleeting, shaped the emotional landscape of the family's migration from Washington to Canada.

Leila's name remains a whisper in the family tree—a reminder of the fragility of frontier life and the sacredness of remembrance.

His death on January 4, 1901, came during a time of transition, likely as the family moved from Washington toward Saskatchewan. No records confirm the cause or burial site, but his name remains etched in the family tree as a symbol of fragility, faith, and remembrance.

Andersons were settling into the Inland Northwest. He grew up surrounded by siblings—

Geneva Josephine Anderson Ervin Born March 28, 1907 – Saint Maries, Benewah County, Idaho Died January 2, 1996 – Calgary, Alberta, Canada Cremated – Ashes given to family or friend.

Geneva was born in the shadow of the St. Joe River, the last child before the arrival of the twins, Netta and Robby. Her early years unfolded in the rhythm of migration—Washington, Idaho, Saskatchewan, and finally Alberta—woven into the Anderson family's northward journey.

Geneva's story is one of quiet continuity. Though few records detail her adult life, her presence in family timelines and memorials affirms her place in Anderson legacy. Her cremation and the private return of her ashes suggest a life remembered intimately, held close by those who knew her best.

Born alongside her twin sister Netta Geraldine "Tootsie" Anderson, Robby entered the world as the youngest daughter of James and Narcissa—a mirrored soul in a family shaped by migration, loss, and enduring love. Her early years unfolded in Washington and Saskatchewan, and after Narcissa's death in 1927, she moved north with James and Netta to British Columbia.

Robby's story is one of quiet devotion and mirrored grace. She witnessed the deaths of all her siblings—Hazel, Blanch, Ernest, Jessie, Grace, and Netta—and carried the Anderson legacy into the northern reaches of Alberta. Her name appears in family records as both "Jeanette" and "Robby," a dual identity that reflects the twin bond she shared with Netta3.

Born August 21, 1889, in Finch, Ontario, Gerald grew up amid Canada's shifting frontiers. He was the son of Archabald Woods and Mary Allice Vance, and half-brother to several Vance siblings through complex family branches. By 1919, he married Hazel Beatrice Anderson, weaving the Anderson lineage into the Wood name.

In 1946, he married Olive Jean Harris, beginning a family line that would carry the Anderson-Wood legacy into American ground. By 1957, Everett had migrated south, entering the U.S. through Blaine, Washington, and eventually settling in Burbank, California, where he became a naturalized citizen in 1965. His name is recorded as "Dr." in some sources—honorary or occupational—a quiet note of distinction.

In 1946, Everett married Olive Jean Harris in Saskatoon. Together they raised a family that included:

Everett immigrated to the United States in 1957, settling in Burbank, California, where he practiced obstetrics and gynecology at St. Joseph's Hospital. He became a naturalized U.S. citizen in 1965, the same year both his parents passed. His life spanned prairie beginnings and Californian legacy, marked by service, family, and quiet resilience.

Born September 10, 1923, in Saskatoon, Saskatchewan, Olive was the daughter of Alexander Harris and Olive Pearl Currie. Raised alongside siblings Nola Dawn, Myrna Gertrude, and John Alexander, she grew up in the heart of prairie Canada, shaped by the rhythms of family and faith.

On September 7, 1946, Olive married Dr. Everett Gerald Wood, son of Hazel Beatrice Anderson and Gerald Clifford Wood. Together they raised a family that included:

Olive immigrated to the United States in 1948, settling in Sunland, California, where she lived for five decades. Her life was marked by quiet resilience, devotion to family, and a gentle strength that anchored her children through transitions and migrations.

In 1969, Janice married Emil Joseph Walcek, a vibrant soul from Indiana and California whose artistic spirit matched her own. Together they founded EJW Associates, Inc. in 1982—a family-run business devoted to marketing, print, and creative collaboration. Their partnership was one of love, laughter, and shared purpose.

A deep devotion to family, legacy, and storytelling

In 1982, Emil founded EJW Associates, Inc., a family-run business rooted in marketing, print, and design. He was a cyclist, artist, thinker, and community activist, known for his infectious smile and tireless generosity. His work shaped trail maps, signage, and advocacy efforts across Roswell and Alpharetta, Georgia.

They met in California, two seekers with different maps—one drawn in prairie ink, the other in mountain trails. They built a life of color, of print and pedal, of children and grandchildren, of stories told and stories still unfolding. They founded a business, a family, a legacy. They gave generously, lived creatively, and loved deeply.

Genealogical Introduction

the Anderson Line:

The descendants of Andrew Berry Anderson (1822–1899), born in Cowan, Franklin County, Tennessee, and laid to rest in Tekoa, Whitman County, Washington. He was one of many children of Peter Anderson Sr. (1765–1824) and Sinai Cynthia Roberts (1781–1874), whose legacy touched Tennessee, Georgia, Arkansas, Missouri, and Washington.

Andrew Berry's marriage to Adeline Elizabeth Dickens (1825–1910) produced a prolific line of children—many of whom lived lives both remarkable and quiet, from Union County, Georgia to the hills of Arkansas and beyond.

Among their children were:

Mary Ann Sina Anderson (1844–1944)

Christopher Columbus Anderson (1846–1925)

John Morton Anderson (1849–1940)

Edward Frost Anderson (1851–1947)

George Washington Anderson (1856–1948)

James Henry Anderson (1866–1957) ...and several others whose brief lives and early losses shaped the emotional terrain of this family's story.

The Anderson line includes soldiers of the Civil War, pioneers of the American frontier, and witnesses to extraordinary change—from horse trails to railroads, from candlelight to electricity.

It is through the grace of shared memory, prayerful research, and the work of cousins known and newly found that this lineage has been uncovered, refined, and preserved. The chapters to follow explore this family's journey with reverence and poetic care—honoring the names etched in stone and the voices that still echo in our lives.

Peter Anderson Sr. (19 Feb 1765 – 12 Jan 1824) Born in New Sweden, Delaware • Laid to rest in Cowan, Tennessee

Origins & Migration

Peter Anderson Sr. entered the world amid colonial uncertainty in New Sweden, Delaware—a place marked by deep Scandinavian roots. Baptized in Wilmington in 1766, his early life unfolded in proximity to rivers, trade routes, and tides of migration. Following family paths and opportunity, he eventually settled in Franklin County, Tennessee, where he would plant enduring roots.

Family & Legacy

Married Sinai Cynthia Roberts around 1800, Peter fathered nine children, many of whom carried his name, spirit, and sense of devotion far beyond Tennessee:

John Watson Anderson (1806–1879)

Peter Anderson Jr. (1808–1876)

Edward Frost Anderson (1810–1862)

William C. Anderson (1812–1862)

Mae Anderson (1814–1814)

Cornelious Robert Benton Anderson (1815–1894)

Daughter (1819–?)

Andrew Berry Anderson (1822–1899)

Catherine Anderson (1824–1895)

His journey echoed through generations who bore his name into Arkansas, Missouri, Washington, and Georgia.

Spiritual Resonance

"Thou shalt not remove thy neighbor's landmark, which they of old time have set."
("King James Version (KJV) - King James Bible Online") — Deuteronomy 19:14

Peter's life became a landmark in and of itself, his burial in Cowan a testament to permanence, faith, and family.

Chapter One (continued)

Sinai Cynthia Roberts (5 June 1781 – 31 August 1874) Born in Botetourt County, Virginia • Passed at Battle Creek, Marion County, Tennessee

Early Life & Family

Sinai entered life amid the ridges of Botetourt County, Virginia, born to Cornelius Neal Roberts, Captain (1749–1788) and Mary Ellen "Polly" Benton (1750–1840). One of many children, she grew up with a legacy steeped in service and frontier grit. Her siblings included Archibald Roberts, Isaac Roberts, Mary Mourning Roberts, and others whose names spread through Virginia, Kentucky, and beyond.

When she lost her father in 1788 near Black Mountain, Russell County, he had been ginseng hunting and was overtaken and scalped by Benge, an Indian, of mixed ancestry. Sinai was just seven—a moment that shaped the course of her resilience.

Marriages & Motherhood

Around 1800, Sinai married Peter Anderson Sr., and together they built a household in Franklin County, Tennessee. Their children—nine strong—were vessels of legacy, faith, and migration. After Peter's passing in 1824, Sinai later married John Bowers Sr. (1773–1848), continuing her journey through decades of change and sorrow, grace, and survival.

She witnessed the Civil War, buried children, and lived to the age of 93, passing in Battle Creek, Marion County, a region now rich with Anderson roots.

Legacy & Reflection

"She looks well to the ways of her household and eat not the bread of idleness." ("Proverbs 31:27-29 ESV - She looks well to the ways of her - Bible Gateway") — Proverbs 31:27

Sinai Cynthia Roberts is the silent strength behind every Anderson branch—her longevity, faith, and endurance echo like a hymn through these pages.

Chapter Two

John Watson Anderson (25 March 1806 – 27 December 1879) Firstborn of Peter Sr. • Settled in Hillsboro, Coffee County

Life & Location

Born in Franklin County, John came of age in a household shaped by frontier values, faith, and hard labor. After marrying Sarah Jane Darnell (1811–1880), he rooted himself in Hillsboro, where his name appears across land records, census rolls, and community memory.

His final resting place in Hillsboro, Coffee County, TN situates him within the region's spiritual and genealogical landscape—near siblings, children, and sites that define the Anderson story.

Children of John Watson & Sarah Jane

Virginia Anderson (1831–1881)

Andrew Lewis Anderson (1833–1900)

Sinah L. Anderson (1835–1914)

Samuel Anderson (b. 1837)

James W. Anderson (1839–1900)

Alexander Peter Anderson (1841–1880)

George W. Anderson (b. 1843)

Orlenia Anderson (1844–1908)

Nathaniel Hamilton Anderson (1845–1919)

Elizabeth Anderson (1847–1906)

Florence Jane Anderson (1855–1949)

Sally Anderson (b. 1857)

John also fathered Henderson Talley (1831–1905) with May or Martha (b. 1800), a woman enslaved prior to emancipation—a truth that anchors this narrative in both familial depth and historical weight.

Service & Legacy

In 1847, John served during the Mexican American War, receiving rank and recognition noted in regional military records. Though quiet in character, his life was not small, it was rooted, branched, and carried forward through thirteen children and more than five decades of change.

Reflection

"Blessed is the man whose delight is in the law of the Lord; he shall be like a tree planted by streams of water." — Psalm 1:2–3

John's life stretches like a tree across Tennessee soil, his name echoing in census lines, grave markers, and living memory. This is my line, Brian Keith Anderson, the storyteller.

Chapter Three

Peter Anderson Jr. (28 November 1808 – 17 January 1876) Born in Cowan • Rooted across Tennessee

Life Threads

Peter Jr., the second son of Peter Sr. and Sinai, was born in Cowan, Franklin County—a cradle of Anderson beginnings. Like his father and brothers, he married young, worked hard, and fathered a large brood of Tennesseans who branched out over time.

Marriages & Family

His life journey included marriages to:

Lucretia Dixon (1809–1850)

Sally Matthews (married 1839 in McMinn County)

Elizabeth Fillers (b. 1817)

With these unions, Peter Jr. had children including:

Arva Sina Anderson (1827–1915)

Allison Anderson (b. 1832)

Mary Ellen Anderson (1835–1881)

James Elmore Anderson (1837–1927)

Francis Cordelia Anderson (b. 1839)

Josiah Anderson (b. 1839)

Records show residences in Jackson, Alabama (1830), and later Green County, Kentucky (1850)a sign of frontier fluidity and the westward pull.

Complexity & Character

Peter Jr.'s timeline is marked by perseverance amid shifting family structures. His marital transitions and geographic mobility reflect both frontier uncertainty and resilience. The repetition of family names like "Elmore" and "Cordelia" hint at spiritual or ancestral tributes.

Reflection

"The lines are fallen unto me in pleasant places; yea, I have a goodly heritage." ("Psalm 16:6-8 KJV - The lines are fallen unto me in - Bible Gateway") — Psalm 16:6

Peter Jr.'s name recurs through multiple counties and branches—a quiet patriarch whose descendants ripple into Coffee, McMinn, Montgomery, and beyond.

Chapter Four

Edward Frost Anderson (1810 – 20 October 1862) Born in Cowan, Tennessee • Lost at Gainesville, Texas

Origins & Migration

Edward Frost was born into the legacy of Peter Sr. and Sinai—part of the sturdy branch rising from Franklin County. His life journey took him westward, settling eventually in Cooke County, Texas. Married to Nancy Matilda Farris (1812–?), he fathered a line of children across Tennessee, Arkansas, and Texas, reflecting both the movement and momentum of the Anderson name.

Descendants of Edward & Nancy

William Anderson (1831–1862)

George W. Anderson (1835–1862)

Jesse M. Anderson (1837–1899)

Susan E. Anderson (b. 1845)

Margaret A. Anderson (b. 1847)

Thomas D. Anderson (b. 1849)

His sons William and George also perished in October 1862, marking this month as one of profound loss for the family.

The Great Hanging of Gainesville

Edward was one of over 40 men accused of Unionist sympathies and executed without trial, mob violence in wartime Texas. Though the records vary, Edward's name remains tethered to this tragedy, symbolizing the cost of conscience during civil unrest.

This brutal act, cloaked as justice, claimed not only Edward but two of his sons, tearing through the Anderson family line with stunning force.

Reflection

"Let justice roll down like waters, and righteousness like an ever-flowing stream." ("Amos 5:24 ESV - But let justice roll down like waters ...") — Amos 5:24

Edward's story is more than a statistic—it is a wound in Texas soil and a whisper across Anderson memory. His life—and the injustice of his death—deserve remembrance, not erasure.

Chapter Five

William C. Anderson (1812 – 13 October 1862) Born in Cowan, Franklin County • Lost at Bridgeport, Texas

Origins & Family Ties

The fifth son of Peter Sr. and Sinai, William, was born in the shadow of the Cumberland foothills, amid the rhythm of a frontier life steeped in family and faith. His siblings stretched across Tennessee and beyond, each a thread in the expanding Anderson legacy.

William's life followed the westward migration of his brothers—settling eventually in Wise County, Texas, where he lived and worked as tensions around Unionist sympathies grew.

The Great Hanging of Texas

On October 13, 1862, William became one of dozens executed in Cooke and Wise Counties during the Great Hanging at Gainesville—a grim episode in Texas Civil War history. Accused without fair trial, he, like his brother Edward Frost Anderson and nephew George W. Anderson, fell to mob violence rooted in fear and political upheaval.

His death in Bridgeport, Wise County is recorded among one of the darkest weeks for the Anderson family, and for justice denied.

Reflection

"Precious in the sight of the Lord is the death of His saints." — Psalm 116:15

William's story is not about one man—it is about conscience, loss, and the power of remembrance. His name, etched in Texas soil, now rises again in these pages.

Chapter Six

Mae Anderson (1814–1814) An infant soul laid to rest in Cowan.

Life and Loss

Born in Tennessee in the year 1814, Mae was the seventh child of Peter Sr. and Sinai Cynthia Roberts. Her life spanned mere months, and yet her name endures among Anderson memory—proof that no life is too short to be honored.

She passed later that same year in Cowan, Franklin County, surrounded by kin who would carry her name forward through generations.

Though records hold only her dates, we may imagine the hush of mourning and the prayers whispered over her grave silence now spoken into your manuscript with love and intention.

30

Reflection

"Before I formed thee in the belly I knew thee." ("Jeremiah 1:5 KJV - Before I formed thee in the belly I - Bible Gateway") — Jeremiah 1:5

Mae reminds us that every soul matters. Her name holds space in the Anderson line, a bloom that opened briefly beneath Tennessee skies.

Chapter Seven

Cornelious Robert Benton Anderson (1815 – 3 April 1894) Born in Cowan • Passed in Bath County, Kentucky

Journey Through States and Sorrows

Cornelious, the sixth son of Peter Sr. and Sinai, entered life in the wooded foothills of Cowan, Franklin County, TN, in 1815. His migration path mirrors the unfolding map of the American frontier: from Tennessee to Arkansas, then to Texas, and finally Kentucky, where he passed at the age of 79.

Through grief and growth, he built two families and raised children whose names carried forward in Texas deeds, Arkansas census rolls, and Kentucky burial grounds.

Marriages & Family

Cornelious married twice:

First Marriage (~1832): to Unknown McGrady

Sinai/Sina L. Anderson (1835–?)

Eliza C. Anderson (1838–1898)

Ann Elizabeth "Eliza" Anderson Thomas (1839–1897)

Unknown son (1839–1840)

Wife and son passed by 1840.

Second Marriage (30 June 1844): to Nancy Askins (1826–1922)

Edward W. Anderson (1845–?)

William Duke Anderson (1847–1929)

John M. Anderson (1851–?)

Texas Anderson (1854–?)

His children were born in Crawford County, Arkansas and Lamar County, Texas, reflecting decades of frontier resilience.

A Brother Among Losses

The year 1862 brought heartbreak. Cornelious lost Edward Frost Anderson and William C. Anderson—two brothers swept up in the tragedy of the Great Hanging in Texas. Their deaths reverberated through family memory, and Cornelious's name stands beside theirs now in solemn kinship.

Final Years & Legacy

Cornelious's closing chapter unfolded in Bath County, Kentucky, far from the Cowan soil of his youth, yet still tethered to the Anderson story. His descendants lived on through farming, preaching, and quiet devotion—echoes of his steady spirit.

"They shall not be ashamed that wait for me." — Isaiah 49:23

Chapter Eight

Daughter Anderson (1819 – unknown) An Anderson child remembered in silence.

Life and Lineage

Born in Franklin County, Tennessee in 1819, this daughter of Peter Sr. and Sinai Cynthia Roberts entered the world between Mae (1814) and Andrew Berry (1822). Though her name is not preserved in surviving records, her birth situates her as the eighth child in a family shaped by faith, endurance, and sorrow.

The absence of marriage, children, or known burial sites leaves us only with her existence—marked by a single line in time, and a quiet space in the tree.

Reflection

""Are not five sparrows sold for two farthings, and not one of them is forgotten before God?"" ("Luke 12:6" Are not five sparrows sold for two pennies? Yet not one of ...") ("The Price of Sparrows - The Institute for Creation Research") — Luke 12:6

Though history did not keep her name, your manuscript does. She is not lost—she is named by remembrance.

Chapter Nine

Andrew Berry Anderson (9 April 1822 – 30 August 1899) Born in Cowan, Tennessee • Laid to rest in Tekoa, Washington

Frontier Pathway

Andrew Berry, youngest son of Peter Sr. and Sinai, was born in the Tennessee hills with legacy already behind him and destiny ahead. He married Adeline Elizabeth Dickens (1825–1910) in Franklin County in 1841, and together they raised thirteen children, some born under southern skies, others cradled by western soil.

His migration trail began in Georgia, moved through Arkansas and Missouri, and ended in Whitman County, Washington, where he passed at age 77.

Children of Andrew & Adeline

Mary Ann Sina Anderson (1844–1944)

Christopher Columbus Anderson (1846–1925)

Sarah J. Anderson (1847–1952)

Cornelius Anderson (1848–1863)

John Morton Anderson (1849–1940)

Edward Frost Anderson (1851–1947)

Cornelius Anderson II (1852–1864)

Andrew Jackson Anderson (1853–1863)

Sarah Elizabeth Anderson (1855–1952)

George Washington Anderson (1856–1948)

Nancy Jane Anderson (1858–1940)

William Dawson Anderson (1861–1937)

James Henry Anderson (1866–1957)

His descendants lived through war, westward expansion, and agricultural upheaval—each carrying names that paid homage to heritage: Columbus, Jackson, Washington, Frost.

Sorrow & Strength

In 1862, Andrew Berry lost brothers Edward Frost and William C. Anderson to the Great Hanging in Texas wound that reverberated across miles. The following year, he lost two sons, Cornelius and Andrew Jackson, and in 1864, another son, Cornelius II. Whether to war, sickness, or sorrow, the losses were devastating.

Still, Andrew pressed forward, eventually settling in Tekoa, Washington, where he would end his days surrounded by family.

Reflection

"They wandered in deserts, and in mountains, and in dens and caves of the earth." ("Hebrews 11:38 The world was not worthy of them. They wandered in ...") — Hebrews 11:38

Andrew Berry Anderson may have wandered farther than any Anderson before him, but never aimlessly. His legacy is one of endurance, remembrance, and grace across geography.

Chapter Ten

Catherine Anderson (5 June 1824 – 21 March 1895) Youngest child of Peter Sr. and Sinai • Matriarch of Tate Cove

Life & Marriage

Catherine was born in Cowan, Franklin County, Tennessee, the twelfth and final child of Peter 1820–1914), planting the roots of a family line that would come to define Tate Cove and the surrounding lands of Marion County.

She spent her life in Tennessee, raising children, enduring immense loss, and remaining a quiet pillar of faith and resilience through seven decades of family history.

Children of Catherine & Rev. Samuel Milton Tate

Sinai Americus Tate (1845–1876)

Rachel Tennessee Tate (1847–1883)

Matilda Ann Tate (1848–1877)

John Knox Tate (1850–1912)

Abigail Clara "Abbie" Tate (1852–1896)

Margaret Angeline Tate (1854–1937)

David McNalley Tate (1857–1945)

Virginia Comfort Tate (1859–1901)

James Bricy Tate (1861–1869)

Joseph Tate (1873–1879)

Her children's names often echoed ancestral honor: Sinai Americus for her mother, Virginia and Tennessee for home soil, Knox, and McNalley for regional ties. The Tate family became woven into Marion County's spiritual, agricultural, and civic fabric.

Sorrow & Resilience

Catherine lived through the losses of at least five children, as well as the deaths of Edward Frost, William C., Peter Jr., Cornelious, and John Watson—siblings whose lives were stilled by violence, distance, and age. And in 1874, she said farewell to her mother Sinai.

Still, Catherine endured with grace. Her name appears in census records from 1850 to 1880, consistently rooted in District 10, Marion County. Her final resting place at Martin Springs Cemetery binds her story to the land where she sowed so much love.

Reflection

"Her children rise up and call her blessed; her husband also, and he praised her." ("Proverbs 31:28 Her children rise up and call her blessed; her husband ...") ("Proverbs 31:28 Her children rise up and call her blessed; her husband ...") — Proverbs 31:28

Catherine's legacy lives in Tate Cove soil, in the names of those she bore, and in the quiet devotion passed from Anderson's daughter to Tate matriarch.

Andrew Berry and Adeline Dickens Anderson

"Andrew Berry and Adeline Elizabeth Dickens Anderson -   steady as the trail, solemn as the promise. From Cowan's foothills to Washington's wheat fields, their portrait opens a journey of faith, loss, and enduring love.

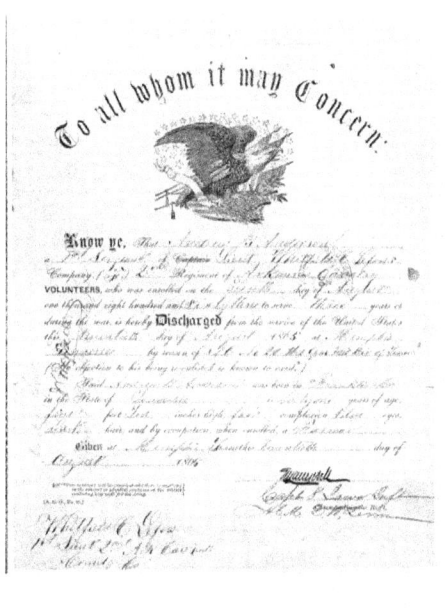

Honor Bound: The Farewell at Memphis August 7, 1865

The war had ended, but not the weight it left behind. At the banks of the Mississippi, under the sweltering Memphis sun, First Sergeant Andrew B. Anderson was handed his discharge-a thin sheet of paper that bore years of grit, grief, and sacrifice. Enlisted at just twenty-one, with blue eyes and dark hair framing a fair face, he had served the Union as part of the 2nd Arkansas Cavalry, under Captain Whitfield's Company F.

Three years earlier, Andrew had been a farmer in Franklin, Tennessee, sowing crops, and dreams. Now he stood as a soldier returned, no longer cradling a plow but the silent testimony of battles survived. His service record, signed by Captain E. Isaac Rolfe, marked not just an end, but a beginning—the path back to soil, family, and peace.

His height—five foot four—might have seemed modest beside other men, but in courage, he towered. The official paper listed no objection to re-enlistment, though Andrew would instead rejoin the rhythms of Tennessee life. Yet the cavalry's dust never fully settled; it lived on in stories shared on porches and in legacy volumes like yours.

And there, tucked in the folds of your manuscript, this discharge will be more than a relic. It will be the quiet heartbeat of a soldier named Anderson—remembered.

A House Split, But Not Broken Franklin County, Tennessee – 1861

The Anderson homestead saw no cannon fire, yet it bore the deepest wounds—three sons at war, but on opposing sides. Andrew Berry Anderson, the youngest of the trio, pledged himself to the Union cavalry. His two elder brothers joined the Confederacy, carrying Tennessee's cause with them into battlefields scarred by conviction and consequence.

Letters from the front were rare. But in one still-kept scrap, Andrew wrote, "I do not hate my brothers, nor they me. We fight as duty calls—but heaven knows our mother's prayers reach us both."

Though their coats bore assorted colors, the Anderson boys were bound by blood, memory, and the land they loved. After Appomattox, it was not politics that stitched them back together—but plowshares, shared pews, and the quiet forgiveness of time.

The Cannon's Echo: A Daughter Remembers Manchester, Tennessee – Circa 1860s

"My father, John Watson, wore gray," she said, her voice steady but distant, as if reaching back through the smoke of memory. "He believed in the South; in the land he tilled and the people he knew. But he never believed in hate."

She was just a girl when the war came to Manchester. The cannons roared like thunder over the hills, and Union soldiers marched through the streets with orders and urgency. Her father had already gone—enlisted with the Confederate Army, leaving behind a wife, children, and a home that would soon be threatened.

"I remember the day they came," she said. "Yankee soldiers gave us fifteen minutes to gather what we could. My mother cried over the family clock, packed with jewelry and money. We tried to save it, but it burned with the house."

What they did save was a rolling pin—wooden, worn, and now sacred. Her father returned after the war, changed but not broke. He never spoke much of battles, but he prayed louder than before. And when he passed, she kept his stories alive—not in bitterness, but in reverence.

From Cowan to Cavalry: The Union Path of Andrew B. Anderson Springfield, Missouri – August 10, 1863

At forty-one, Andrew Berry Anderson was no fresh-faced recruit. Born in Franklin County, Tennessee, in 1822, he had already weathered the loss of two sons and two brothers to the war's toll. Yet on that summer day in Springfield, Missouri, he stepped forward and enlisted as a private in Company F of the 2nd Arkansas Union Cavalry—a regiment formed in defiance of secession, drawn from pockets of loyalty scattered across the Ozarks.

His muster took place in Arkansas, where the regiment would serve in skirmishes, scouting missions, and guerrilla suppression across Newton, Searcy, Izard, and Carroll counties. Andrew's rise to First Sergeant spoke not just to rank, but to resilience. He was a farmer turned soldier, a Tennessean fighting for the Union while his brothers wore Confederate gray.

The 2nd Arkansas Cavalry was the only Arkansas Union regiment to counter Sterling Price's Missouri Raid from start to finish. In 1865, they were transferred to the east of the Mississippi, serving in Tennessee and Mississippi until the war's end1. Andrew survived it all, and in 1890, he applied for a pension—a quiet acknowledgment of service rendered, and sacrifice endured.

His story is not just one of military record. It is the story of a man who chose conviction over comfort, unity over division. And in your manuscript, Brian, it becomes a thread in the greater quilt of Anderson legacy—stitched with honor.

Adeline of the Trail: A Mother's Resolve Born June 10, 1825 – Greene County, Georgia Died December 10, 1910 – Nez Perce County, Idaho

Adeline Elizabeth Dickens married Andrew Berry Anderson in Franklin County, Tennessee, in the spring of 1841. She was just sixteen, with dark eyes and a steady heart. Together, they would raise thirteen children—some born in Georgia, others in Arkansas, and still more in Missouri—each arrival marking another chapter in their westward migration.

She buried three sons during the Civil War years: Cornelius, Andrew Jackson, and a second Cornelius, all lost before their twelfth birthdays. Her husband fought for the Union while his brothers wore Confederate gray. Adeline held the home together, stitching quilts, tending gardens, and praying through cannon fire and silence.

From the hills of Union County to the plains of Arkansas and the valleys of Washington State, Adeline moved with grace and grit. She saw the birth of railroads, the rise of statehoods, and the fading of frontier life. Her final years were spent in Tekoa, Washington, where she was laid to rest beside Andrew in Goldenrod Cemetery.

Her legacy lives in the hands of her daughters, the laughter of her grandchildren, and the quiet strength passed down through generations. She was not just a wife or mother—she was the matriarch of a migration, the keeper of memory, and the soul of the Anderson story.

Children of Andrew Berry and Adeline Elizabeth Anderson
Spanning Georgia, Arkansas, Missouri, and Washington

Mary Ann Sina Anderson Wimpy: A Century Rooted in Grace Born June 7, 1844 – Blairsville, Georgia Died May 17, 1944 – Nez Perce County, Idaho

Born in the mountain town of Blairsville, Georgia, Mary Ann Sina Anderson was the eldest daughter of Andrew Berry Anderson and Adeline Elizabeth Dickens. Her childhood was steeped in frontier rhythms—quilts stitched by candlelight, hymns sung in pinewood churches, and the slow westward pull of family migration.

She witnessed the Civil War as a young girl, losing three brothers—Cornelius, Andrew Jackson, and a second Cornelius—before their twelfth birthday. Her father fought for the Union, her uncles for the Confederacy. Through it all, Mary Ann remained a quiet anchor, helping her mother tend to the younger children and carry the family's faith forward.

In 1867, she married Thomas Jefferson Wimpy in Benton County, Arkansas. Together they raised a large family, with children born in Georgia, Arkansas, and Washington—each birth marking another step in the Anderson migration. By 1880, she had settled in Spangle, Washington, and later in Nez Perce County, Idaho, where she lived out her final decades.

Mary Ann outlived all her siblings, including her youngest brother James Henry Anderson, and passed away just shy of her 100th birthday. Her burial in Lewiston, Idaho, closed a century-long chapter that began in the red clay of Georgia and ended in the wheat fields of the Northwest.

Christopher Columbus Anderson: From Georgia Pines to California Shores Born August 4, 1846 – Union County, Georgia Died November 2, 1925 – Vallejo, Solano County, California

Named for the explorer who crossed oceans, Christopher Columbus Anderson crossed a continent. Born in the Appalachian foothills of Union County, Georgia, he was the second child of Andrew Berry and Adeline Anderson. His early years were shaped by the rhythms of frontier life—plowing fields, tending livestock, and watching his family grow as they migrated westward.

By the 1860s, Christopher had witnessed the heartbreak of war. Three younger brothers—Cornelius (twice) and Andrew Jackson—died during the Civil War years. His father fought for the Union, while uncles stood with the Confederacy. Christopher himself would marry Salina C. Asbell in Missouri in 1866, and together they raised a large family across Missouri and Washington.

Eventually, Christopher settled in Vallejo, California, where he worked as a machinist helper and lived out his final years. He died in 1925, having seen the country transform from wagon trails to railroads, from divided states to a unified nation.

His life was one of quiet endurance—marked not by fame, but by family, labor, and legacy. And in your manuscript, Brian, he becomes more than a name. He becomes a bridge between generations.

Sarah J. Anderson Huffman: A Century of Quiet Strength Born circa 1847 – Arkansas Died December 30, 1952 – Tekoa, Whitman County, Washington

Born in the shadow of the Civil War, Sarah J. Anderson was one of the earliest children of Andrew Berry and Adeline Elizabeth Anderson. Her birth in Arkansas marked the family's westward shift from Georgia, and her life would mirror the migration that defined the Anderson legacy.

She married George F. Huffman in Nez Perce County, Idaho, in 1880, and together they raised a family that would settle deep roots in the Pacific Northwest. Sarah lived through the deaths of her parents, her siblings, and the transformation of Tekoa from a frontier town to a settled community. She outlived all her siblings—including Mary Ann Sina, Christopher Columbus, and George Washington Anderson—and bore witness to the passing of three Cornelius's brothers and Andrew Jackson, all lost young.

Sarah's final years were spent in Tekoa, where she died at the age of 105. Her burial in Goldenrod Cemetery placed her beside the very soil that her family helped pioneer. Her long life was marked not by headlines, but by endurance, grace, and the quiet rhythm of family.

Cornelius Anderson: A Life Cut Short, A Legacy Remembered Born February 18, 1848 – Union County, Georgia Died January 13, 1863 – Fayetteville, Washington County, Arkansas

Cornelius was the third child of Andrew Berry and Adeline Elizabeth Anderson, born in the red clay hills of Union County, Georgia. His early years were spent among the rhythms of a growing family—siblings arriving in quick succession, the household migrating westward through Arkansas and Missouri, chasing farmland and hope.

By 1863, the Andersons had settled near Fayetteville, Arkansas, a region torn by Civil War. Cornelius was just fourteen when he died, a casualty of the conflict's collateral toll—disease, displacement, or the violence that swept through Washington County during the war's fiercest years. His burial in Evergreen Cemetery places him among the earliest Andersons laid to rest in western soil.

Though he never reached adulthood, Cornelius's name lives on in family memory. His parents would name another son Cornelius in 1852, only to lose him as well in 1864. These twin losses—two sons bearing the same name—speak to both grief and remembrance, a mother's longing, and a father's sorrow.

In your manuscript, Brian, Cornelius becomes more than a footnote. He becomes a symbol of the cost of war, the fragility of frontier life, and the enduring love of a family that carried his name westward.

John Morton Anderson: The Quiet Pioneer of Rosalia Born July 27, 1849 – Union County, Georgia Died December 25, 1940 – Rosalia, Whitman County, Washington

John Morton Anderson was the sixth child of Andrew Berry and Adeline Elizabeth Anderson, born in the Appalachian foothills of Union County, Georgia. His early years were sha father who fought for the Union, and a mother who held the family together through sorrow and soil.

By 1873, John had married Virginia Bell Jones, and together they raised four children: Joseph, Rhoda J., John Jr., and Dora Belle. Their journey took them from Arkansas to

Washington, where John settled in Rosalia, Whitman County town nestled among wheat fields and railroad tracks.

He worked on the land, raised his family, and lived to see the deaths of all his siblings. His final years were spent in quiet reflection, surrounded by the legacy he helped build. On Christmas Day, 1940, at the age of 91, John passed away in Rosalia. He was buried in the IOOF Evergreen Cemetery, close to the soil his family had tilled for generations.

Edward Frost Anderson: The Settler Who Carried the Flame Born February 17, 1851 – Union County, Georgia Died May 9, 1947 – Clarkston, Asotin County, Washington

Edward Frost Anderson was the fifth child of Andrew Berry and Adeline Elizabeth Dickens Anderson, born into a family already shaped by migration and mourning. His early years unfolded in Georgia and Arkansas, where he witnessed the loss of three younger brothers—Cornelius (twice) and Andrew Jackson—during the Civil War years. His father fought for the Union, his uncles for the Confederacy, and Edward grew up in the shadow of both conviction and consequence.

In 1871, Edward married Emma Elizabeth Bozarth in Benton County, Arkansas. Together they had several children before Emma's death in 1887. Two years later, Edward married Keturah Hannah Belle Masterson in Lewiston, Idaho, and their union produced a large family—fourteen children in total, born across Arkansas, Washington, and Idaho.

Edward's life was one of movement and making:

He lived in Spangle, Washington, in 1880, and later in Nez Perce and Clarkston, Idaho and Washington.

He worked the land, raised children, and buried loved ones—including sons Benton and Clarence, and daughters Minnie and Edna.

He applied for a pension in 1890, a quiet testament to his service and survival.

He lived to see the deaths of all his siblings, including Mary Ann Sina, John Morton, and Christopher Columbus. His final years were spent in Clarkston, Washington, where he died at the age of 96 and was buried in Vineland Cemetery.

Andrew Jackson Anderson Born April 5, 1853 – Arkansas Died 1863 – Age 10

Born into the growing family of Andrew Berry and Adeline Elizabeth Dickens Anderson, Andrew Jackson was the sixth child and part of a generation shaped by frontier hardship fed by Civil War unrest. His birth in Arkansas marked a westward shift for the Andersons, who had left Georgia behind in search of new beginnings.

Though his life was short, Andrew's presence was felt among his siblings—Sarah Elizabeth, George Washington, Nancy Jane, and William Dawson—each of whom would live long lives and carry forward the family name. His death in 1863, at just ten years old, came during a time of national upheaval, and though the cause is unknown, the loss was surely felt deeply by his parents and siblings.

Andrew's memory lives quietly in the family tree, a reminder of the fragility of childhood in a turbulent era. His name, shared with a famous general and president, suggests the hopes his parents may have held for him—a life of strength, leadership, and legacy.

George Washington Anderson Born October 31, 1856 – Bloomfield, Benton County, Arkansas Died August 27, 1948 – Spokane, Spokane County, Washington Buried – Latah Cemetery, Spokane County, Washington

The seventh child of Andrew Berry and Adeline Elizabeth Dickens Anderson, George Washington, was born in Bloomfield, Arkansas, during a time of expansion and uncertainty. He came of age amid the Civil War and the loss of younger siblings, including Andrew Jackson and Cornelius.

George married Cora Maria Harvey in 1882 in Spokane, Washington. Together they raised four children:

Elmer Ernest Anderson (b. 1882)

Clay Berry Anderson (1886–1963)

Dulcie May Anderson (1895–1960)

Delta Maud Anderson (1905–1906), who died in infancy.

George's life was rooted in the Inland Northwest:

He lived in Latah, Spokane County, and later in Benewah County, Idaho

He served as a County Sheriff, a role that reflected his sense of order and community

He worked on the land and raised a family through decades of change—from horse-drawn wagons to automobiles

He outlived his wife Cora by 25 years and witnessed the passing of all his siblings, including Edward Frost, Sarah Elizabeth, and Christopher Columbus. George died at age 91 and was laid to rest in Latah Cemetery, where the wheat fields meet the sky.

James Henry Anderson Born December 4, 1866 – Springfield, Greene County, Missouri Died January 7, 1957 – Abbotsford, British Columbia, Canada Buried – Hazelwood Cemetery, Abbotsford

The youngest son of Andrew Berry and Adeline Elizabeth Dickens Anderson, James Henry, was born in Springfield, Missouri, as the family continued its westward journey. By age three, he was living in Benton County, Arkansas, and by his teens, he had settled in Spangle, Washington—part of the Anderson migration to the Inland Northwest.

James Henry's wife:

Narcissa Ellen Hunter Anderson Born May 8, 1868 – Corner Springs, Benton County, Arkansas Died June 30, 1927 – Biggar, Saskatchewan, Canada Buried – Biggar Memorial Gardens Cemetery, Saskatchewan

Born in the Ozark foothills of Arkansas, Narcissa Ellen was the daughter of Thomas Hunter. By 1880, she was living in Neosho, Missouri, listed as a boarder alongside her sister Maggie—a glimpse into a childhood shaped by movement and modest means[3].

In 1891, she married James Henry Anderson in Spokane, Washington. Together they raised a large family across Washington, Idaho, and Canada. Her children included:

Ernest Leroy Anderson (1892–1974)

Grace Ellen Anderson (1894–1978)

Blanch Mabel Anderson (1895–1970)

Hazel Beatrice Anderson (1899–1965)

Jessie Minnie Anderson (1904–1976)

Geneva Josephine Ervin (1907–1996)

Netta Geraldine "Tootsie" Anderson (1909–1976)

Jeanette "Robby" Anderson (1909–1987)

Plus, four children lost in infancy: Lula B., Leila B., an unnamed infant son, and an unnamed infant daughter.

Narcissa's journey took her from the American South to the wheat fields of Saskatchewan. She arrived in British Columbia in 1910, and by 1916 was living in Biggar, where she died in 1927 at age 59. Her burial in Biggar Memorial Gardens marks the final resting place of a woman whose legacy stretches across borders and generations[1].

Ernest Leroy Anderson Born June 5, 1892 – Tekoa, Whitman County, Washington Died October 10, 1974 – Burns Lake, British Columbia, Canada Buried – Burns Lake Municipal Cemetery, Bulkley-Nechako District, BC

Ernest was the firstborn of a large and scattered family, arriving in Tekoa just as the Andersons were settling into the Inland Northwest. He grew up surrounded by siblings—Grace, Blanch, Hazel, Jessie, Geneva, and the twins Netta and Robby—as well as the quiet grief of lost infants: Lula B., Leila B., and unnamed brothers and sisters.

His journey included:

Residences in Waverly, Colfax, and Spokane, Washington

A northward migration to Saskatchewan and British Columbia by 1916

Marriage to Charlotte Walker in 1920, followed later by Muriel E., with at least one daughter, Eileen Anderson Toombs

Work across Oregon, Washington, and Canada, including time in Portland and Seattle

A quiet passing in Burns Lake at age 82, having outlived both parents and many siblings

Ernest's life was one of quiet movement and enduring ties. He carried the Anderson name into Canada, where it took root in new soil. His burial in Burns Lake marks the northernmost point of the Anderson migration—a place where the legacy settled and bloomed.

Grace Ellen Anderson McClure Born July 26, 1894 – Tekoa, Whitman County, Washington Died December 6, 1978 – Abbotsford, British Columbia, Canada Buried – Hazelwood Cemetery, Abbotsford

Grace was born in the Palouse hills of Washington, just a year after her brother Ernest. She grew up in a bustling household of siblings—Blanch, Hazel, Jessie, Geneva, and the twins Netta and Robby—alongside the quiet grief of lost infants: Lula B., Leila B., and unnamed brothers and sisters.

Her life unfolded across decades and borders:

She married three times—first to Alfred "Alf" Worthington, then to Stan Dibley, and finally to Herb McClure, whose name she carried to her grave

She migrated with the family to Saskatchewan and British Columbia, settling in Abbotsford where she lived out her final years

She outlived both parents and many siblings, passing away at age 84

migration and mourning—three younger brothers lost during the Civil War, a

Grace's story is one of quiet endurance and layered identity. Her multiple marriages suggest resilience and reinvention, while her burial in Hazelwood Cemetery places her firmly in the Canadian branch of the Anderson legacy.

Blanch Mabel Anderson Mackenzie Born April 23, 1895 – Latah, Spokane County, Washington Died February 14, 1970 – Saskatoon, Saskatchewan, Canada Buried – Woodlawn Cemetery, Saskatoon

Blanch was born into a growing family, nestled between Grace and Hazel, and surrounded by both joy and sorrow. Her early years in Washington were marked by the births and losses of siblings—Lula B., Leila B., and an unnamed infant son—all of whom passed in infancy. She grew up alongside Hazel, Jessie, Geneva, and the twins Netta and Robby, forming a sisterhood that would stretch across borders.

Her journey included:

Migration with the family to Saskatchewan, by the 1910s

Marriage to [Mr. Mackenzie], surname confirmed by burial records

A quiet life in Saskatoon, where she passed away at age 74

7 Burial in Woodlawn Cemetery, Block 32A, Lot L128, Section NH

Blanche's story is one of gentle continuity—no known children, but a life lived in the rhythm of family migrations and prairie seasons. Her name appears in family records as a steady presence, and her burial in Saskatoon places her among the northern Anderson branches.

Lula B. Anderson Born October 1898 – Washington State Died August 1, 1900 – Revelstoke, British Columbia, Canada Buried – [location not yet confirmed]

Lula B. was born into the Anderson family during their years in Washington, nestled between Blanch and Hazel in birth order. Her arrival marked the eighth child of James and

Narcissa, and her presence—though fleeting—was part of the rhythm of a family constantly on the move.

Her death in Revelstoke at just under two years old came during the family's northward migration, enroute to Saskatchewan. The cause is unknown, but the timing suggests hardship amid travel, illness, or the strain of frontier life.

Though Lula B. left no descendants, her name remains stitched into the Anderson quilt— an echo of innocence and loss. Her memory is honored alongside siblings who lived long lives and those, like Leila and the unnamed infants, whose stories were brief but sacred.

##

Hazel Beatrice Anderson

Hazel and Gerald Clifford Wood

Hazel Beatrice Anderson Wood Born October 24, 1899 – Latah, Spokane County, Washington Died December 17, 1965 – Victoria, British Columbia, Canada Buried – Royal Oak Burial Park, Victoria

Hazel was born into a rhythm of migration and memory, arriving just a year after the loss of her sister Lula B. and amid the births and deaths of other infant siblings—Leila B., an unnamed infant son, and later an unnamed infant daughter. She grew up surrounded by sisters—

Blanch, Grace, Jessie, Geneva, and the twins Netta and Robby—each carrying a thread of the Anderson legacy.

Her journey included:

Migration with the family from Washington to Saskatchewan and eventually British

Marriage to Gerald Clifford Wood around 1919

Raising three children in Biggar, Saskatchewan:

Everett Gerald Wood, Dr. (1920–2004)

Donald John Wood (1921–1978)

Geneva Geraldine Wood (1922–1999)

A quiet passing in Victoria at age 66, laid to rest in Royal Oak Burial Park

Hazel's life was one of homemaking, devotion, and quiet strength. She outlived her mother Narcissa by four decades and witnessed the passing of her father James in 1957. Her children carried the Anderson name into medicine, community, and memory.

Leila B. Anderson Born 1900 – Latah, Spokane County, Washington Died 1900 – Age less than one year Burial – [location not yet confirmed]

Leila B. was born into a season of both growth and grief. Her arrival followed the loss of Lula B. in 1900 and preceded the birth of Hazel Beatrice later that same year. Though her life was brief and no records confirm the exact date or cause of death, her presence is stitched into the Anderson lineage with quiet reverence.

She was one of four infants lost to James and Narcissa—alongside Lula B., an unnamed son, and an unnamed daughter. These little lights, though fleeting, shaped the emotional landscape of the family's migration from Washington to Canada.

Leila's name remains a whisper in the family tree—a reminder of the fragility of frontier life and the sacredness of remembrance.

Infant Son Anderson Born December 24, 1900 – [Washington or in route to Canada] Died January 4, 1901 – Age 11 days Burial – [location not yet confirmed]

Born on Christmas Eve, this unnamed son entered the world during a season of migration and mourning. His birth followed the loss of Lula B. and Leila B. and preceded the arrival of Hazel Beatrice later that same year. Though his life lasted only eleven days, his presence was deeply felt in the Anderson household—a fleeting light amid the long journey northward.

His death on January 4, 1901, came during a time of transition, likely as the family moved from Washington toward Saskatchewan. No records confirm the cause or burial site, but his name remains etched in the family tree as a symbol of fragility, faith, and remembrance.

Geneva Josephine Anderson Ervin Born March 28, 1907 – Saint Maries, Benewah County, Idaho Died January 2, 1996 – Calgary, Alberta, Canada Cremated – Ashes given to family or friend.

Geneva was born in the shadow of the St. Joe River, the last child before the arrival of the twins, Netta and Robby. Her early years unfolded in the rhythm of migration—Washington, Idaho, Saskatchewan, and finally Alberta—woven into the Anderson family's northward journey.

Her life included:

A childhood shaped by movement and memory, following the loss of infant siblings and the strength of older sisters

Marriage to [Mr. Ervin], surname confirmed by memorial records

A quiet passing in Calgary at age 88, having outlived both parents and all siblings

Geneva's story is one of quiet continuity. Though few records detail her adult life, her presence in family timelines and memorials affirms her place in Anderson legacy. Her cremation and the private return of her ashes suggest a life remembered intimately, held close by those who knew her best.

Netta Geraldine "Tootsie" Anderson Kless Born November 30, 1909 – Colfax, Whitman County, Washington Died May 1976 – Grande Prairie, Alberta, Canada Buried – City of Grand Prairie Cemetery, Alberta

Born alongside her twin sister Jeanette "Robby" Anderson, Netta entered the world as the ninth daughter of James and Narcissa—two bright threads woven into the final stretch of the Anderson migration. Her early years unfolded in Washington and Saskatchewan, shaped by the loss of her mother in 1927 and the quiet strength of her father, who moved with the twins to British Columbia.

Netta's life included:

Three marriages: Jack McCarty, James Harold McGillvery, and Ralph Kless

Mother to nine children, including:

Infant McCarty (1930–1930)

Doreen (1934–2018)

Jeanette (b. 1936)

Robert (1938–1963)

Edward Kless (1944–1955)

Ione, Loraine, Valerie, and Phill Kless

Her journey was one of resilience and reinvention—marked by loss, love, and the quiet labor of motherhood. She outlived many siblings, including Ernest, Hazel, Blanch, and Jessie, and passed away in Grand Prairie at age 66. Her burial in the City of Grand Prairie Cemetery places her firmly in the northern branch of the Anderson legacy.

Jeanette "Robby" Anderson Gray Born November 30, 1909 – Colfax, Whitman County, Washington Died 1987 – Grande Prairie, Alberta, Canada Buried – City of Grand Prairie Cemetery, Alberta

Born alongside her twin sister Netta Geraldine "Tootsie" Anderson, Robby entered the world as the youngest daughter of James and Narcissa—a mirrored soul in a family shaped by migration, loss, and enduring love. Her early years unfolded in Washington and Saskatchewan, and after Narcissa's death in 1927, she moved north with James and Netta to British Columbia.

Her life included:

Marriage to [Mr. Gray], surname confirmed by memorial records

A quiet life in Grand Prairie, Alberta, where she outlived her twin over a decade

A passing in 1987 at age 77 or 78, laid to rest in the City of Grand Prairie Cemetery

Robby's story is one of quiet devotion and mirrored grace. She witnessed the deaths of all her siblings—Hazel, Blanch, Ernest, Jessie, Grace, and Netta—and carried the Anderson legacy into the northern reaches of Alberta. Her name appears in family records as both "Jeanette" and "Robby," a dual identity that reflects the twin bond she shared with Netta3.

Hazel Beatrice Anderson, daughter of James Henry and Narcissa Ellen, standing in grace and quiet strength. From her gaze, a legacy unfolds.

Gerald Clifford Wood (1889–1965)

Born August 21, 1889, in Finch, Ontario, Gerald grew up amid Canada's shifting frontiers. He was the son of Archabald Woods and Mary Allice Vance, and half-brother to several Vance siblings through complex family branches. By 1919, he married Hazel Beatrice Anderson, weaving the Anderson lineage into the Wood name.

Gerald's migrations carried him from Ontario to Manitoba to Saskatchewan and finally to Victoria, British Columbia, where he died on December 19, 1965. He is buried at Royal Oak Burial Park, just two days after Hazel's passing—a testament to a life bound in love and legacy.

Gerald's legacy flows through Everett to Janice Dawne Wood Walcek, grounding her in prairie soil and eastern timber.

Dr. Wood

Everett Gerald Wood, Dr. (1920–2004)

Born March 31, 1920, in Biggar, Saskatchewan, Everett was the son of Hazel Beatrice Anderson and Gerald Clifford Wood. Raised on prairie soil, he came of age during Canada's interwar years, working as a teamster by 1940 and settling briefly in Saskatoon.

Olive Jean Harris Wood

In 1946, he married Olive Jean Harris, beginning a family line that would carry the Anderson-Wood legacy into American ground. By 1957, Everett had migrated south, entering the U.S. through Blaine, Washington, and eventually settling in Burbank, California, where he became a naturalized citizen in 1965. His name is recorded as "Dr." in some sources—honorary or occupational—a quiet note of distinction.

He fathered several children, including:

Everett died on April 1, 2004, in Burbank, and was laid to rest in Hollywood Hills, completing a life that spanned prairies, borders, and blended traditions.

Donald John Wood (1921–1978)

Born February 12, 1921, in Biggar, Saskatchewan, Donald was the second child of Hazel Beatrice Anderson and Gerald Clifford Wood. Raised alongside Everett and Geneva, his early years were shaped by prairie life and postwar transitions. Records show him residing in the Leion district of Biggar by June 1921.

Donald remained rooted in Saskatchewan, passing away on December 19, 1978, in Saskatoon, just as his father had thirteen years earlier. He was laid to rest at Woodlawn Cemetery in Saskatoon—a quiet resting place that echoes the soil of his birth.

His life, though less documented than Everett's, still carries the thread of Hazel's legacy and Gerald's migrations. Donald's presence in the manuscript becomes a steady stitch—one that holds the prairie quilt together.

Geneva Geraldine Wood (1922–1999)

Born August 30, 1922, in Biggar, Saskatchewan, Geneva was the youngest child of Hazel Beatrice Anderson and Gerald Clifford Wood. Raised alongside Everett and Donald, she spent her early years in Rosetown and St. Andrews districts, shaped by prairie rhythms and postwar transitions.

In 1963, Geneva married Hugh James Norrie, and later, after 1976, she wed James Edgar Hawke, extending the Wood-Anderson legacy into new branches. She remained rooted in Saskatchewan, passing away on February 21, 1999, in Saskatoon, and was laid to rest at Woodlawn Cemetery, where her brother Donald also rests.

Geneva's life was one of quiet continuity—her name stitched into prairie soil, her story echoing Hazel's grace, and Gerald's migrations. She carried the thread forward with dignity, even as the quilt expanded.

Dr. Everett Gerald Wood (1920–2004)

Born March 31, 1920, in Biggar, Saskatchewan, Everett was the eldest child of Hazel Beatrice Anderson and Gerald Clifford Wood. Raised on prairie soil, he came of age during Canada's interwar years, working as a teamster by 1940 and later studying medicine.

In 1946, Everett married Olive Jean Harris in Saskatoon. Together they raised a family that included:

Janice Dawne Wood Walcek (1948–2019)

Joann Wood (1951–2004)

Michael John Wood (1961–2007)

Susan, Darcy, David, and others carrying Hazel's thread forward.

Everett immigrated to the United States in 1957, settling in Burbank, California, where he practiced obstetrics and gynecology at St. Joseph's Hospital. He became a naturalized U.S. citizen in 1965, the same year both his parents passed. His life spanned prairie beginnings and Californian legacy, marked by service, family, and quiet resilience.

He passed away on April 1, 2004, in Burbank, and was laid to rest at Forest Lawn Memorial Park, Hollywood Hills.

Olive Jean Harris (1923–2004)

Born September 10, 1923, in Saskatoon, Saskatchewan, Olive was the daughter of Alexander Harris and Olive Pearl Currie. Raised alongside siblings Nola Dawn, Myrna Gertrude, and John Alexander, she grew up in the heart of prairie Canada, shaped by the rhythms of family and faith.

On September 7, 1946, Olive married Dr. Everett Gerald Wood, son of Hazel Beatrice Anderson and Gerald Clifford Wood. Together they raised a family that included:

Janice Dawne Wood Walcek (1948–2019)

Joann Wood (1951–2004)

Michael John Wood (1961–2007)

Susan, Darcy, David, and others carrying Hazel's thread forward.

Olive immigrated to the United States in 1948, settling in Sunland, California, where she lived for five decades. Her life was marked by quiet resilience, devotion to family, and a gentle strength that anchored her children through transitions and migrations.

She passed away on March 9, 2004, in Burbank, California, just weeks before Everett, and was laid to rest at Forest Lawn Memorial Park, Hollywood Hills 2.

"She was a seeker. A seeker of stories. A seeker of ancestors. Through her seeking, she found me— Brian Keith Anderson, a man with dusty records, weathered photos, and a heart for remembering. I am just a storyteller. But Janice? She stitched soul to story and made me part of the tale."

Janice Dawne Wood Walcek (1948–2019)

Born April 8, 1948, in Saskatoon, Saskatchewan, Janice was the daughter of Dr. Everett Gerald Wood and Olive Jean Harris, and granddaughter of Hazel Beatrice Anderson and Gerald Clifford Wood. She grew up in Sunland, California, where prairie roots met Pacific light.

In 1969, Janice married Emil Joseph Walcek, a vibrant soul from Indiana and California whose artistic spirit matched her own. Together they founded EJW Associates, Inc. in 1982—a family-run business devoted to marketing, print, and creative collaboration. Their partnership was one of love, laughter, and shared purpose.

Janice was a devoted mother to:

Erin married Matthew.

Sean, married to Lisa.

Heather, married to Patrick.

She was also a proud grandmother to Killian, Ian, Annabel, Chloe, and Lilian—each a living echo of Hazel's thread.

Janice passed away peacefully on November 21, 2019, in Roswell, Georgia, and was cremated at Northside Chapel Crematory2. Her life was marked by:

A passion for genealogy, reading, and road trips across North America

A deep devotion to family, legacy, and storytelling

A quiet strength that stitched prairie memory into modern grace

Janice Walcek Obituary

WALCEK, JANICE DAWNE JANICE DAWNE

WALCEK (N?E WOOD), 71, OF ROSWELL PASSED

AWAY PEACEFULLY ON NOVEMBER 21, 2019.

SHE WAS BORN ON APRIL 8, 1948, IN

SASKATOON

WALCEK, Janice Dawne Janice Dawne Walcek , Wood), 71, of Roswell passed away peacefully on November 21, 2019. She was born on April 8, 1948, in Saskatoon, Saskatchewan, Canada, to Olive and Everett Wood. She grew up in Sunland, Los Angeles, where she met and wed Emil Joseph Walcek in 1969. They moved to Atlanta in 1972. After working in the medical industry, she became the co-owner of EJW Associates, Inc. with Emil in 1982. Janice was a devoted wife and mother to three energetic kids, with a passion for working in the family business, genealogy, reading, and road trips across the country and Canada. Survived by daughter Erin and son-in-law Matthew, son Sean and daughter-in-law Lisa, daughter Heather and son-in-law Patrick, grandchildren Killian, Ian, Annabel, Chloe, and Lilian, brother David, and sisters Susan and Darcy. Preceded in death by her husband, her sister Jo Ann, her brother Michael, and her parents.

Saskatchewan, Canada, to Olive and Everett Wood. She grew up in Sunland, Los Angeles, where she met and wed Emil Joseph Walcek in 1969. They moved to Atlanta in 1972. After working in the medical industry, she became the co-owner of EJW Associates, Inc. with Emil in 1982. Janice was a devoted wife and mother to three energetic kids, with a passion for working in the family business, genealogy, reading, and road trips across the country and Canada. Survived by daughter Erin and son-in-law Matthew, son Sean and daughter-in-law Lisa, daughter Heather and son-in-law Patrick, grandchildren Killian, Ian, Annabel, Chloe, and Lilian, brother David, and sisters Susan and Darcy. Preceded in death by her husband, her sister Jo Ann, her brother Michael, and her parents.

Emil Joseph Walcek Jr. (1948–2019)

Obituary:

Born October 21, 1948, in South Bend, St. Joseph County, Indiana, Emil was the son of Emil Walcek Sr. and Kathleen Schrom Walcek. He grew up in Tujunga, California, where he met and married Janice Dawne Wood in 1969, a union of inventive minds and kindred spirits.

In 1982, Emil founded EJW Associates, Inc., a family-run business rooted in marketing, print, and design. He was a cyclist, artist, thinker, and community activist, known for his infectious smile and tireless generosity. His work shaped trail maps, signage, and advocacy efforts across Roswell and Alpharetta, Georgia.

Emil passed away on March 6, 2019, in Roswell, Georgia, from injuries sustained in a cycling collision2. He was cremated at Northside Chapel Crematory, where a memorial service was held on March 16, 2019.

He is remembered by:

His wife, Janice

Children: Erin (Matthew), Sean (Lisa), Heather (Patrick)

Grandchildren: Killian, Ian, Annabel, Chloe, Lilian

Siblings: John, Joseph, Christopher, Edward, Mary, Theresa, Rosie, Annie

Preceded in death by his mother, Kathleen.

"The Final Stitch: Janice & Emil's Benediction

The End of the Tale: Janice and Emil

They met in California, two seekers with different maps—one drawn in prairie ink, the other in mountain trails. They built a life of color, of print and pedal, of children and grandchildren, of stories told and stories still unfolding. They founded a business, a family, a legacy. They gave generously, lived creatively, and loved deeply.

Janice sought ancestors. Emil sought horizons. Together, they found each other. And through Janice's seeking, she found Brian Keith Anderson, a storyteller drawn into the quilt they stitched.

Now their tale is told. But the thread continues— in Erin, Sean, Heather, in Killian, Ian, Annabel, Chloe, and Lilian, in every map Emil drew, in every name Janice uncovered.

This is not the end. It is binding. The final stitch. The quiet amen.

Index

Abbie 37

Abbotsford 18, 50, 52, 53

Abigail 37

Abigail Clara 74

Accused 31

Addressing 2

Adeline 14, 15, 16, 17, 18, 23, 35, 39, 43, 44, 45, 46, 49, 74

Adeline Elizabeth 13, 16, 17, 47, 48

Adeline Elizabeth Anderson 15, 46

Adeline Elizabeth Dickens 14, 35, 43, 50

Adeline Elizabeth Dickens Anderson 39, 49

After 26, 41, 69, 70

After Peter 25

Alabama 28

Alberta 20, 59, 60, 61

Alexander 21, 27, 65, 66, 74, 78

Alexander Harris 74

Alfred 5

All Hesitations 2

Allice 20

Allison 74

Allison Anderson 28

Alpharetta 22, 71

America 5, 68

American 21, 23, 27, 32, 63

American South 51, 74

American War 74

Americus 81

Among 23, 33, 75

Amos 30

And Anderson 34

Anderson Born October 74

Anderson Ervin Born March 20, 59

Anderson Huffman 74

Anderson Kless 74

Anderson Line 22

Anderson Springfield 74

Anderson Thomas 74

Andersons 17, 20, 47, 49, 52

Andrew 1, 4, 10, 12, 13, 14, 15, 16, 17, 18, 22, 23, 24, 26, 34, 35, 36, 39, 40, 41, 42, 44, 46, 48, 49, 50, 74, 83

Andrew Berry 2, 12, 13, 14, 15, 16, 17, 34, 36, 39, 41, 45, 46, 47, 48, 49, 50

Andrew Berry Anderson 14, 43, 83

Andrew Jackson 16, 17, 43, 45, 46, 49

Andrew Jackson Anderson 35

Andrew Lewis Anderson 74

Andrews 64

Angeles 69

Angeline 79

Ann Elizabeth 33, 74

Ann Sina 49

Ann Sina Anderson 35, 44, 79

Annabel 68, 70, 72, 73

Annie 72

Appalachian 9, 15, 16, 45, 47

Appomattox 41

April 12, 32, 34, 49, 63, 65, 67, 69

Archabald 20

Archabald Woods 62, 74

Archibald Roberts 25, 74

Arkansas 10, 14, 15, 16, 17, 18, 22, 23, 24, 29, 32, 33, 35, 42, 43, 44, 46, 47, 48, 49, 50, 51, 74, 83

Arkansas Cavalry 40, 42

Arkansas Died August 49

Arkansas Died June 51

Arkansas Union 42

Arkansas Union Cavalry 14

Arkansas Union Regi 83

Army 41

Around 25

Arva 28, 75

Asbell 15, 45

Ashes 20, 59

Askins 33, 80

Asotin County 48, 75

Associates 22, 68, 69, 70, 71

Atlanta 69, 70

August 12, 25, 34, 39, 41, 45, 54, 64, 83

Baptized 10, 24

Bath 12, 33

Bath County 32, 75

Battle 26

Battle Creek 25, 75

Beatrice 21, 51, 56, 61, 62, 66, 67, 78

Beatrice Anderson 63, 64, 65

Before 32

Bell Jones 47

Belle 17, 48, 79

Bend 71

Benediction 73

Benewah 20, 50, 59, 75

Benge 25

Benton 17, 24, 25, 32, 48, 49, 51, 76

Benton County 14, 18, 44, 50, 75

Berry 1, 4, 10, 12, 13, 14, 16, 17, 18, 22, 23, 24, 34, 35, 36, 39, 40, 44, 46, 49, 74

Beth 4, 9, 75

Bible 3, 13, 26

Bible Gateway 29, 32

Biggar 51, 58, 62, 63, 64, 65, 75

Biggar Memorial 51

Biggar Memorial Gardens 51

Black Mountain 25, 75

Blaine 21, 63

Blairsville 14, 44

Blanch 18, 19, 20, 52, 53, 54, 58, 60, 61, 75

Blanch Mabel 51

Blanch Mabel Anderson Mackenzie Born April 54

Blanche 19, 54

Blessed 27

Block 54

Bloomfield 49

Born 12, 14, 15, 17, 20, 24, 25, 26, 28, 29, 30, 31, 32, 34, 41, 43, 44, 45, 46, 47, 48, 49, 50, 51, 52, 54, 58, 59, 60, 61, 62, 63, 64, 65, 67, 71, 74, 83

Born August 20, 62

Born September 21, 65

Botetourt 25

Botetourt County 75

Bound 39

Bowers 78

Bozarth 17, 48, 77

Brian 1, 2, 5, 15, 16, 42, 46, 47, 67, 73

Brian Keith Anderson 27, 75

Bricy 78

Bridgeport 11, 30, 31

British 18, 19, 20, 51, 52, 53, 57, 58, 61

British Columbia 50, 52, 54, 60, 62, 75

Brother 33, 75

Brother Among Losses 7

Bulkley 52

Burbank 21, 63, 65, 66

Burial 54, 58, 59

Burial Park 57, 62

Buried 52, 54, 57

Burns 7, 52, 75

Burns Lake 52

Burns Lake Municipal 52

But Janice 67

But Not Broken 40

Calgary 7, 20, 59

California 21, 22, 45, 63, 65, 66, 67, 68, 71, 73

Californian 21, 65

Canada 18, 19, 20, 21, 51, 52, 54, 57, 58, 59, 62, 65, 66, 69, 70

Canada Buried 50, 51, 52, 54, 60, 61

Canadian 54

Captain 13, 25, 40

Captain Whitfield 40, 75

Carried 48

Carroll 42

Carthage 13

Catherine 12, 36, 37, 38, 75

Catherine Anderson 24

Cavalry 41, 42, 74, 83

Cemetery 7, 16, 37, 46, 47, 49, 52, 54, 61, 63, 75, 77, 78, 79, 81, 82

Century 44, 46

Chapel 72, 80

Chapter Eight 7, 75

Chapter Five 75

Chapter Four 6, 75

Chapter Nine 7, 75

Chapter One 75

Chapter Seven 75

Chapter Six 76

Chapter Ten 76

Chapter Three 6, 76

Chapter Two 6, 76

Character 28

Charlotte 52, 76

Chat 4

Children 26, 35, 36, 44, 72

Chloe 68, 70, 72, 73

Christmas 17, 48, 59

Christopher 15, 23, 35, 45, 46, 50, 72, 76

Christopher Columbus 15, 45, 49

Circa 41

City 7, 60, 61

Civil 16, 17, 23, 26, 31, 47, 48, 49, 50, 53, 81

Civil War 14, 15, 43, 44, 45, 46

Clara 37

Clarence 48

Clarkston 48, 49

Clay Berry 50

Clay Berry Anderson 76

Clifford 57, 61

Clifford Wood 67

Coffee 11, 29

Coffee County 26, 76

Colfax 52, 60, 61

Columbia 18, 19, 20, 51, 52, 53, 57, 61

Columbus 12, 16, 23, 35, 45, 46, 50, 76

Comfort 82

Company 83

Company 14, 40, 42, 83

Complexity 28

Confederacy 13, 14, 15, 17, 40, 44, 45, 48

Confederate 41, 42, 43, 83

Cooke 29, 31

Cooke County 76

Copyright 5

Cora 50, 76

Cordelia 11, 29

Cornelious 11, 12, 24, 32, 33, 37, 76

Cornelius 14, 15, 16, 17, 25, 36, 43, 44, 45, 46, 47, 48, 50, 76

Cornelius Anderson 35

Corner 51

Counties 31

County 7, 11, 12, 14, 15, 16, 17, 20, 22, 25, 28, 29, 30, 31, 33, 34, 36, 37, 40, 41, 43, 45, 46, 47, 48, 49, 50, 51, 52, 58, 59, 60, 61, 71, 75, 78, 80

County Sheriff 76

Cowan 4, 10, 12, 22, 24, 25, 28, 29, 30, 31, 32, 33, 34, 36, 39, 41, 83

Crawford 33

Crawford County 76

Creation Research 34

Creek 26

Cremated 20, 59

Crematory 72, 80

Cumberland 11, 30

Currie 21, 65, 80

Cynthia 12, 24, 25, 26, 34, 79

Cynthia Roberts 31

Darcy 65, 66, 70

Daughter 24, 34, 41, 76

David 37, 65, 66, 70

Dawn 21, 65

Dawne 62, 65, 66, 67, 69, 78

Dawson 17, 49, 82

December 26, 50, 52, 57, 59, 62, 63

Delaware 10, 24

Delta 50

Delta Maud Anderson 76

Descendants 11, 29

Deuteronomy 25

Dickens 14, 17, 18, 23, 39, 44, 48, 49, 74

Died 20, 49, 52, 54, 57, 58, 59

Died December 43, 46

Died January 50, 59

Died November 45

Disclosure 5

District 37

Dixon 28

Donald 58, 63, 64, 76

Donald John Wood 8

Dora Belle 47, 76

Doreen 60

Duke 33

Dulcie 50

Dulcie May Anderson 76

Each 9

Early 11, 25

Early Life 6

Echo 41

Edgar 64

Edna 48

Edward 11, 17, 24, 29, 30, 31, 33, 35, 37, 48, 50, 60, 72, 76

Edward Frost 17, 29, 36, 48

Edward Frost Anderson 23

Edward Kless 76

Eight 34

Eileen 77

Eileen Anderson Toombs 52

Eliza 33

Elizabeth 14, 16, 17, 18, 23, 44, 46, 48, 49, 50, 74, 77, 81

Elizabeth Anderson 27

Elizabeth Fillers 28, 77

Ellen 51, 52, 61

Elmer 77

Elmer Ernest Anderson 50

Elmore 11, 28, 29, 78

Emil 3, 4, 7, 8, 22, 68, 69, 70, 71, 72, 73, 77

Emil Joseph Walcek 69, 70

Emil Walcek Sr 71, 77

Emma 17, 48, 77

Enlisted 39

Erin 68, 69, 70, 72, 73

Ernest 18, 20, 52, 53, 60, 61, 77

Ernest Leroy Anderson 51, 77

Ervin 59

Eventually 45

Everet 7

Everett 8, 21, 62, 63, 64, 65, 66, 67, 69

Everett Gerald Wood 58, 77

Everett Wood 70

Evergreen 47

Evergreen Cemetery 17, 48, 77

Family Ties 10

Fayetteville 46, 47, 83

February 46, 48, 54, 63, 64

Finally 7, 33, 73

Finch 20, 62

First 83

First Edition 5

First Marriage 33

First Sergeant 42, 83

First Sergeant Andrew 39, 77

Firstborn 26

Five 6, 30

Flame 48

Florence 27

Florence Jane Anderson 77

Following 10, 24

Forest 65, 77

Forest Lawn Memorial Park 66

Four 29

Francis Cordelia Anderson 28, 77

Franklin 12, 13, 14, 22, 30, 31, 34, 36, 40, 41

Franklin County 10, 14, 24, 25, 26, 28, 29, 32, 35, 43, 77, 83

From 39, 41, 43, 45, 61, 83

Frontier 34

Frontier Pathway 7, 77

Frost 11, 12, 24, 29, 31, 33, 35, 37, 48, 50, 76

Gainesville 6, 29, 30, 31

Gardens 75

Gardens Cemetery 51

Gateway 26

Genealogical 6, 22

Genealogical Introduction 77

Geneva 18, 20, 52, 53, 54, 58, 59, 60, 63, 64

Geneva Geraldine Wood 8, 77

Geneva Josephine 20, 59

Geneva Josephine Ervin 51, 77

George 11, 15, 16, 17, 23, 27, 29, 30, 31, 35, 46, 49, 50, 77

George Washington Anderson 46

Georgia 10, 14, 15, 16, 17, 22, 23, 24, 35, 43, 44, 45, 46, 47, 48, 49, 68, 71, 72

Georgia Died December 47

Georgia Died January 46

Georgia Died May 44, 48

Gerald 8, 20, 21, 57, 61, 62, 64, 66, 67

Gerald Clifford Wood 7, 21, 58, 62, 63, 64, 65, 66, 77

Gerald Wood 8

Geraldine 51, 58, 60, 64, 80

Gertrude 21, 65

Goldenrod 16, 46

Goldenrod Cemetery 44, 77

Grace 18, 20, 44, 52, 53, 54, 58, 61

Grace Ellen Anderson 51, 77

Grand 7, 60, 61, 77, 78

Grand Prairie 61

Grand Prairie Cemetery 61

Grandchildren 72

Grand Prairie 60, 61

Gray 61, 74

Great 31, 33, 36

Great Hanging 11, 78

Green 28, 78

Greene 43, 50

Guided 9

Hamilton 27, 80

Hanging 6, 30, 31, 33, 36

Hannah 17, 48, 79

Harold 60

Harris 21, 65

Harvey 50, 76

Hawke 64

Hazel 18, 19, 20, 21, 51, 52, 53, 54, 56, 57, 58, 60, 61, 62, 63, 64, 65, 66, 67, 68, 78

Hazel Beatrice 58, 59

Hazel Beatrice Anderson Wood Born October 57

Hazelwood 54

Hazelwood Cemetery 50, 52, 78

Heather 68, 69, 70, 72, 73

Hebrews 36

Henderson Talley 27, 78

Henry 10, 18, 23, 50, 51, 61

Herb 53

Hills 63

Hillsboro 26

Hollywood 63

Hollywood Hills 65, 66, 78

Honor 39

Hospital 21, 65

House 40

Huffman 15, 46

Hugh 64

Hugh James Norrie 78

Hundred 78

Hunter 51

Idaho 15, 17, 18, 20, 43, 44, 45, 46, 48, 50, 51, 59

Index 74

Indian 25

Indiana 22, 68, 71

Infant 59, 60

Inland 20, 52

Inland Northwest 18, 50

Ione 60

Isaac Roberts 25, 78

Isaac Rolfe 13, 40, 78

Isaiah 34

Izard 42

Jack 60

Jackson 12, 14, 15, 17, 28, 35, 36, 44, 48, 49, 50, 74

James 10, 18, 19, 20, 23, 27, 28, 50, 51, 54, 58, 60, 61, 64, 78

James Bricy Tate 37

James Edgar Hawke 78

James Harold 78

James Henry 45

James Henry Anderson 35, 78

Jane 17, 26, 49

Jane Anderson 27, 80

Janice 3, 4, 7, 8, 9, 22, 62, 65, 66, 67, 68, 69, 70, 72, 73, 78

Janice Dawne Wood 71

Janice Waleck 78

January 19, 20, 28, 59

Jean Harris 21, 63, 65, 67

Jeanette 20, 51, 60, 61

Jefferson 81

Jeremiah 32

Jesse 29

Jessie 18, 20, 52, 53, 54, 58, 60, 61, 78

Jessie Minnie Anderson 51

Jo Ann 70

Joann Wood 65, 66, 78

Joe River 20, 59, 78

John 17, 26, 27, 33, 37, 47, 48, 49, 58, 63, 65, 66, 72, 76, 78, 79, 80

John Alexander 21

John Bowers Sr 25

John Jr 47

John Knox Tate 37

John Morton 16, 35, 47

John Morton Anderson 23

John Watson 41

John Watson Anderson 24

Joseph 7, 8, 21, 22, 37, 47, 65, 68, 71, 72, 77

Joseph County 79

Joseph Tate 79

Josiah 79

Josiah Anderson 28

Journey 7, 32

Journey Through States 79

July 47, 52

June 25, 33, 36, 43, 44, 52, 63

Kathleen 72, 79

Kathleen Schrom Walcek 71

Keith 1, 2, 5, 67, 73

Kentucky 12, 25, 28, 32, 33

Keturah 17, 48, 79

Killian 68, 70, 72, 73

King James Bible Online 25

King James Version 25

Kless 60

Knox 13, 37, 79

Laid 12, 24, 34

Lake 7, 52, 75

Lamar 33

Lamar County 79

Latah 49, 50, 54, 57, 58, 79

Latah Cemetery 50

Latah County 13, 79

Lawn 65, 77

Leila 18, 19, 51, 52, 53, 54, 55, 57, 58, 59

Leion 63

Leroy 52

Letters 40

Lewis 26

Lewiston 17, 45, 48

Life Cut Short 46

Life Threads 6, 28

Like 28

Lilian 68, 70, 72, 73

Lineage 7, 34

Lisa 68, 69, 70, 72

Location 6, 26

Loraine 60

Lord 27, 31

Los Angeles 70

Loss 6, 31

Losses 33, 75

Lost 29, 30

Lucretia 28

Lucretia Dixon 79

Luke 34

Lula 18, 19, 51, 52, 53, 54, 55, 57, 58, 59

Mabel 75

Mackenzie 54

Mae Anderson 24, 31, 79

Maggie 51

Manchester 41, 76

Manitoba 62

March 26, 36, 62, 65, 66, 72

Margaret 29, 79

Margaret Angeline Tate 37

Maria 50, 76

Marion 37

Marion County 12, 13, 25, 26, 36, 37, 79

Marriage 7, 33, 36, 52, 54, 58, 59, 61

Marriages 11, 25, 28, 32

Married 24, 29, 79

Martha 27

Martin 37

Martin Springs Cemetery 79

Mary 20, 35, 44, 45, 49, 72, 79

Mary Allice Vance 62, 79

Mary Ann 14, 44

Mary Ann Sina 15, 46

Mary Ann Sina Anderson 14, 23, 44

Mary Ellen 25

Mary Ellen Anderson 28, 79

Mary Mourning Roberts 25, 79

Masterson 17, 48, 79

Matilda Ann Tate 37, 80

Matriarch 36

Matthew 68, 69, 70, 72

Matthews 28

Maud 50

May Anderson 50

Memorial ,,,,,,,... 75, 77

Memorial Park 65

Memphis 39

Mexican 27

Michael 65, 66, 70, 80

Migration 6, 18, 19, 24, 29, 54, 58

Milton 36

Minnie 48, 78

Mississippi 39, 42, 83

Missouri 10, 13, 14, 15, 16, 18, 22, 24, 35, 41, 43, 44, 45, 47, 50, 51, 83

Missouri Raid 42

Montgomery 11, 29

Morton 47, 49, 79

Mother 43, 60

Motherhood 25

Mountains 4

Municipal 75

Muriel 52

Myrna 21, 65

Myrna Gertrude 80

Named 15, 45

Nancy 11, 17, 29, 33, 49, 80

Nancy Jane Anderson 35

Nancy Matilda Farris 29, 80

Narcissa 19, 20, 51, 55, 58, 60, 61

Narcissa Ellen 51, 80

Nathaniel 27, 80

Neal 25, 76

.... 13

Missouri Raid 42

Montgomery 11, 29

Morton 47, 49, 79

Mother 43, 60

Motherhood 25

Mountains 4

Municipal 75

Muriel 52

Myrna 21, 65

Myrna Gertrude 80

Named 15, 45

Nancy 11, 17, 29, 33, 49, 80

Nancy Jane Anderson 35

Nancy Matilda Farris 29, 80

Narcissa 19, 20, 51, 55, 58, 60, 61

Narcissa Ellen 51, 80

Nathaniel 27, 80

Neal 25, 76

.... 13

Olive 21, 63, 65, 66, 67, 69, 70, 80

Olive Jean Harris 8, 21, 63, 80

In October 31

In September 21, 66

Ontario 20, 62

Oregon 52

Orlenia 27, 80

Ozark 51

Ozarks 14, 42

Pacific 67

Pacific Northwest 15, 46

Palouse 53

Park 7, 77, 80

Passed 25, 32

Path 41, 83

Pathway 34

Patrick 68, 69, 70, 72

Pearl 21, 65, 80

Peter 10, 11, 12, 24, 25, 26, 27, 28, 29, 30, 31, 34, 35, 36, 37, 74, 80

Peter Anderson Jr 24, 80

Peter Anderson Sr 4, 10, 12, 22, 24

Peter Jr 28, 29

Peter Sr 28, 29, 32

Phill 60

Phill Kless 80

Pines 45

Pioneer 47

Plus 51

Polly 25

Portland 52

Prairie 7, 61, 77, 78

Prairie Cemetery 60

Preceded 70, 72

Precious 31

Price 34, 42

Printed 5

Proverbs 3, 26, 37

Psalm 27, 29, 31

Quiet 46

Rachel 37, 80

Raid 83

Raised 21, 62, 63, 64, 65

Raising 58

Ralph 60

Ralph Kless 80

Records 28, 63

Remembered 46

Remember 41, 76

Residences 52

Resilience 7, 37

Resolve 43

Revelstoke 19, 54, 55

Rhoda 47

Robby 18, 20, 51, 52, 53, 54, 58, 59, 60, 61

Robert 24, 32, 60, 76

Roberts 12, 24, 25, 26, 34, 76, 79

Rooted 28, 44

Rosalia 17, 47, 48

Rosetown 64

Rosie 72

Roswell 22, 68, 69, 71, 72

Royal 7, 57, 80

Royal Oak 62

Royal Oak Burial Park 58

Russell County 25, 80

Saint Maries 20, 59, 81

Salina ....,,................................ 15, 45

Sally 28, 81

Sally Anderson 27

Sally Matthews 81

Samuel 36, 81

Samuel Anderson 27

Samuel Milton Tate 12, 81

Sarah 15, 16, 17, 26, 35, 46, 49, 50, 81

Sarah Elizabeth Anderson 35

Sarah Jane Darnell 26, 81

Saskatchewan 18, 19, 20, 21, 51, 52, 53, 54, 55, 58, 59, 60, 61, 62, 63, 64, 65, 67, 69, 70

Saskatoon 7, 19, 21, 54, 62, 63, 64, 65, 67, 69

Saundra 4, 9, 81

Scandinavian 10, 24

Schrom 79

Sean 68, 69, 70, 72, 73

Searcy 42

Seattle 52

Second 33

Section 54

Sergeant 83

Service 6, 27

Settled 26

Seven 7, 32

Sheriff 7, 50

Shores 45

Siblings 72

Sina 33

Sina Anderson 28, 75

Sinah 26

Sinai 11, 12, 24, 25, 26, 28, 29, 30, 31, 32, 33, 34, 35, 36, 37, 79, 81

Sinai Americus 13, 37

Sinai Americus Tate 36

Sinai Cynthia Roberts 10, 12, 22

Solano County 45, 81

Son Anderson 59

Sorrow 7, 35, 37

Sorrows 7, 32

South 41, 71

Spangle 15, 18, 45, 48, 50

Spanning Georgia 44, 81

Sparrows 34

Spiritual Resonance 6, 81

Split 40

Spokane 18, 49, 50, 51, 52, 58, 78

Spokane County 49, 54, 57, 81

Springfield 14, 18, 41, 50, 83

Springs 37, 51

Stan Dibley 53, 81

State 43, 54

States 5, 7, 21, 32, 65, 66

Sterling 42

Sterling Price 81, 83

Still 12, 36, 37

Stitch 73

Strength 7, 35, 46

Sunland 21, 66, 67, 69, 70

Survived 69, 70

Susan 29, 65, 66, 70

Sweden 24

Tale 7, 8, 73

Tate 36, 37, 38, 78, 79, 80, 81, 82

Tate Cove 12, 36, 38, 81

Tekoa 10, 12, 15, 16, 18, 22, 34, 36, 44, 46, 52, 83

Tennessean 42, 83

Tennesseans 28

Tennessee 10, 11, 12, 13, 14, 22, 24, 25, 27, 28, 29, 30, 31, 32, 34, 35, 36, 37, 40, 41, 42, 43, 80, 83

Texas 6, 9, 11, 29, 30, 31, 32, 33, 36, 81

That 83

Anderson 13, 23, 40

The Cannon 41

The Chronicle 13

The End 7, 8, 73

The Family 1, 10

The Farewell 39

The Great .... ,,, 6, 30, 31

The Institute 34

The Quiet 47

The Settler 48

The Tate 13, 37

The Union 41, 83

Their 4, 11, 22, 25, 33, 47, 68

Then 3

Theresa 72

109

These 16, 19, 47, 58

They 9, 13, 22, 34, 36, 69, 70, 73

This 4, 5, 9, 10, 11, 27, 30, 73

Thomas 30, 33, 51, 81

Thomas Hunter 81

Thomas Jefferson Wimpy 14, 44

Thou 25

Though 12, 16, 17, 19, 20, 27, 30, 31, 34, 41, 47, 49, 55, 58, 59, 60

Three 13, 28, 40, 45, 60

Through 7, 14, 32, 44, 67

Ties 6, 11, 30

Together 4, 14, 17, 18, 21, 22, 43, 44, 48, 50, 51, 65, 66, 68, 73

Toombs 77

Tootsie 20, 51, 60, 61

Trail 43

Tujunga 71

Union 13, 14, 15, 16, 17, 40, 41, 42, 43, 44, 45, 46, 47, 48, 74, 83

Union Cavalry 83

Union County 16, 23, 45, 46, 48, 81

Unionist 30

United 5, 21, 65, 66

Unknown 33

Valerie 60

Vallejo 45

Vance 20, 21, 62

Victoria 7, 57, 58, 62

Vineland 81

Vineland Cemetery 49

Virginia 13, 25, 37, 47, 82

Virginia Anderson 26, 81

Virginia Bell Jones 82

Virginia Comfort Tate 37

Wagons 78

Walcek 7, 8, 22, 62, 65, 66, 68, 69, 71, 77, 78, 79

Waleck 4

Walker 52, 76

Washington 10, 12, 13, 14, 15, 16, 17, 18, 19, 20, 21, 22, 23, 24, 34, 35, 36, 39, 43, 44, 45, 46, 47, 48, 49,

50, 51, 52, 53, 54, 57, 58, 59, 60, 61, 63, 77

Washington Buried 49

Washington County 46, 47, 82

Washington Died 61

Washington Died May 60

Watson 26, 37, 79

Waverly 52

What 3, 9, 41

When 4, 25

Whether 36

Whitman 22, 48, 52, 60, 61

Whitman County 10, 35, 46, 47, 82

Wife 33

William 11, 17, 24, 30, 31, 33, 36, 37, 49, 82

William Anderson 29, 82

William Dawson Anderson 35

William Duke Anderson 82

Wilmington 10, 24

Wimpy 44, 81

Winchester 4

Wise 11, 30, 31

Wise Counties 82

Wise County 82

With 9, 28

Wood 8, 21, 57, 58, 61, 62, 63, 64, 65, 66, 67, 69, 76, 78, 80

Wood Walcek 67

Woodlawn 54, 63, 82

Woodlawn Cemetery 64

Woods 20

Work 52

Worthington 53

Yahoo 4

Yankee 14, 41

Years 7, 33

Youngest 36

Your 3

From Cowan to Cavalry:
The Union Path of
Andrew B. Anderson

Springfield, Missouri —August 10, 1863

At forty-one, Andrew serry Anderson was no fres-faced recqruit— Born in Franklin County, Tennessee, in 1822, he id a arady weahered a two sons and two brothers to war's toll — andrew mi berobeered for the Confeclare Union Cavalty—a regimen in Coumpa:y First Sergeant in Compan F-*of*

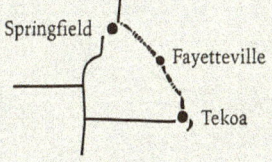

Springfield

Fayetteville

Tekoa

the 2nd Arkansas Union Cavalry. the only Arkansas Union regiment to counter Sterling Price's. Missouri Raid from start to finish. In 1803, serving in Tennessee and Mississippi until the war's end.

Andrew's rise to First Sergeant . a.Prlorrhe, a Tennessean fighting for the Union while his brothers wore Confederate gray.

His story is not just one of one of military record. It's a storisome ane conviction over comfort, unity over division. And when he passed military record. That's the story of a man who chose conviction over comfoct, unity over division. Het satory—bynben5 u, Alaigh—greater quilt of Anderson legacy—not in just one edted suriermbered, but to rewerence.

His story—is one of military record. It's the story of a man who coose conviction over comfort, unity over division. And in your manufictent. Brian, Irlan, applied for a pension:—and even scorda once-atdcks.

115

www.ingramcontent.com/pod-product-compliance
Lightning Source LLC
Chambersburg PA
CBHW020552030426
42337CB00013B/1058